MURDER IN VICTORIAN LIVERPOOL

Murder in
Victorian Liverpool

David Parry

Published by Palatine Books,
an imprint of Carnegie Publishing Ltd
Carnegie House,
Chatsworth Road,
Lancaster, LA1 4SL
www.carnegiepublishing.com

ISBN 978-1-874181-80-4

Designed and typeset by Carnegie Book Production

Printed and bound in the UK by Short Run Press, Exeter

Contents

Introduction

The thirty-three murder cases described in this book came to trial at the Liverpool Assizes within a thirty-year period following the passage of the Capital Punishment Amendment Act of 1868. It was partly due to the campaigning in the national press of prominent opponents of the "grotesque spectacle" of public executions, such as Sir Robert Peel and Charles Dickens, that the reform was enacted. The act required that all prisoners who were sentenced to death should be executed within the walls of the prison in which they were being held, and that their bodies should be buried in the prison grounds. The change from public to private hanging occurred primarily because too many people saw the former as inhumane, and it was also believed that it no longer acted as a deterrent to other criminals. There was also widespread concern at the drunkenness and public disorder that public hangings sometimes generated among the crowds of people that gathered to watch.

The following trials resulted in the conviction and judicial execution of thirty men and five women, two of which were conducted as double hangings. According to the provisions of the new act, all of the hangings were carried out inside the prisons where the convicted men and women had been held.

Whatever you believe about the rights and wrongs of capital punishment, the cases in this book give a fascinating insight into life in the Victorian period, in Liverpool and beyond. Although murder can never be condoned, it is clear from the accounts of the lives of the accused and their victims that the world they inhabited was a harsh one, where people were pushed to the very end of their tethers on a daily basis. It seems little wonder sometimes that people snapped under the strain, and this is clearly what happened in some of the cases described here. Others, however, are much more brutal and premeditated and still have the ability to shock 150 years on.

Paying a Price

On Monday 21st December 1869, John Gregson of Wigan was indicted at Liverpool's St George's Hall for having 'on 18th October last, feloniously, wilfully, and of his malice aforethought, killed and murdered his wife Ellen Gregson'.

If Gregson were to be convicted of murder, he would receive a mandatory sentence of death. Because of the passage of the 1868 Private Executions Act, his sufferings on the gallows at Kirkdale Prison would take place in front of only a few people. He would not have to bear the terrible indignity of being put to death before a crowd of thousands of onlookers.

The Gregsons had two children, and on the day of the murder, the family had attended the police court to pay a fine for drunkenness. John Gregson was well known to the Wigan magistrates, having appeared before them twenty-four times, which resulted in many visits to the county gaol. Ellen Gregson's six years of married life must have been a period of uninterrupted misery; her husband was an ill-tempered and violent criminal, and on several occasions she was obliged to seek the protection of the magistrates.

One evening on 18th October, the Gregsons returned home at around 6.30 pm; a lodger, Maria Hirst, had been looking after the children. John and Ellen had both been drinking and a dispute arose over the pawning of John's jacket in order to pay for more drink. Whilst Ellen took her baby from Maria and began to feed it on the breast, Gregson took off his jacket and asked a neighbour, Mrs Littler, to pledge it at the pawnshop. Agreeing to do so the next day, she placed it on a hook behind the door. Impatiently, Gregson said he would take it himself and took it back off the hook. His wife stood up, snatched the jacket from under his arm, and told him to go and sit on the stairs.

'I will take it myself in a few minutes.' She snapped.

'Look sharp then, and fetch me a pint of beer. If you don't look sharp I'll give you a kicking,' Gregson replied.

'I'll not pawn it for drink, but I will for food.' Ellen retorted.

Eventually, Maria advised Ellen, 'Take the jacket for quietness sake.' Ellen wrapped Gregson's jacket in a shawl, but once again she refused to buy any more drink. At this, Gregson took the baby off Ellen, and, running at her, gave her a hefty kick on the right leg. She fell to the floor and as she was lying there, Gregson continued to run at her with repeated kicks to her legs, chest, back and sides.

'Maria, help me!' She cried. Another neighbour, Bob Hilton, had been in the house when the Gregsons returned home, and hearing the commotion he ran in, grabbing Gregson and pushing him into a chair. He went to Ellen's aid, and as he was lifting her head from the floor, Gregson continued his onslaught. He got up from the chair, and running again at Ellen, kicked at her head, his heavy clogs connecting with her skull, just behind the ear. Ellen's body went rigid, her tongue shot out of her mouth, and blood flowed from both ears.

'Jack, thou hast killed her!' Hilton screamed. To this came Gregson's reply: 'If I haven't I ought to have.'

His anger by now assuaged, Gregson brought a shovel and spread a pile of ashes over the blood that covered the floor. Sticky, dark blood was now flowing copiously from Ellen's mouth as well as her ears. Hilton tried to staunch it using a wet handkerchief and by applying a sticking plaster. Hilton and Maria then carried Ellen to the bedroom.

'She's only acting,' Gregson spat. Meanwhile, Ellen was shouting: 'Murder!' and 'Maria!'

When Maria went to Ellen's bedroom later that night, she found her lying on the bed, undressed. She was vomiting blood. Gregson was in a drunken sleep next to her.

The next morning, on Monday 19th October, Maria went out to her work as usual. When she returned in the evening, Gregson was out, so Maria began to wash the blood off the staircase. While she was doing so, Gregson came back and they both went upstairs to see how Ellen was getting on. Ellen did not reply to her husband's inquiries.

'She can't speak to me, let alone you,' Maria told him.

On the following evening, Dr Jackson came to see Ellen. She was, according to the doctor, 'raving and insensible to everything except pain', continuously shouting 'Maria!' and 'God help my poor head!'

She had sustained a wound under her right ear that had penetrated to the bone. There was bruising around her breasts, arms and body.

Gregson sent for some brandy for her, but she would not drink it; her teeth clenched firmly. She died two nights later on the Thursday evening at around 8.30 pm.

During a cross-examination, Maria Hirst said that the whole attack by Gregson on his wife occupied 'only about four minutes'. About five minutes after the attack, Gregson told Maria to pledge his jacket for ten shillings and pay for a doctor with the money. She did as he asked, but returned to the house and told him she could only get three shillings for it.

Gregson was arrested in the bedroom by Police Constable Bushell. When told that his wife was dead, he replied, 'Then the Lord help me.' The cause of Ellen's death was put down to a fracture to the base of the skull.

At the trial – after the closure by Mr Leresche of the case for the prosecution – Mr Torr rose to address the jury on behalf of Gregson. He claimed that there was no 'murderous intent' on Gregson's part and treated the attack as if it were an everyday occurrence in Wigan.

'Unfortunately, the conduct of which the prisoner has been guilty is not uncommon in some parts of Lancashire,' Torr said. He went on, 'That which is common, although dangerous, and done without impunity more than once or twice, may be done once too often, but by its very commonness may be taken as good evidence that there was no murderous intention on the part of the prisoner.'

According to Torr, there was no reason for supposing that Gregson had intended to kill his wife any more than when he had beaten her on previous occasions. He argued that the crime was not murder, but manslaughter. Gregson, Torr told the jury, was 'totally uneducated, a state of things, perhaps, for which some of you are to a great extent responsible as citizens, and he is brutal in his habits'.

Finally, Torr said, 'The prisoner's love of drink has brought him, as it has brought many others, and will probably bring many more, perhaps some who hear me into an awful position. However, you the jury ought to ask yourselves: Was the prisoner in hot blood when he attacked his wife? Had he lost control of his mind? If you are of that opinion, you ought to take a charitable view of the matter, and not return a verdict which will cause the forfeit of the prisoner's life.'

Summing up, the judge, Baron Martin, told the jury, 'The killing of a person by an unlawful act of violence without excuse or justification, is what the law calls murder. I am bound further to tell the jury that, if they believe the evidence in the case, the crime of which the prisoner is guilty is murder and not manslaughter.'

The jury had difficulty in reaching an unanimous verdict. Two jurymen had doubts as to whether or not a murder had been committed. One of them asked the judge whether it was murder, if, at the time Gregson gave the fatal blow, he intended to 'reduce his wife to subjection' and not to kill her. The judge replied: 'If he gave the blow, and she died, that would be murder. A man must take the consequences of an unlawful act of that sort.'

Baron Martin, apparently exasperated by the jurymen's repeated questions, declared: 'I thought no human being could mistake me, and I told you, that if you believe that what these persons have sworn is the truth, then the crime that this man is guilty of is, by law, murder.'

Baron Martin said that if the jury wished it, he would read over all of the evidence again, but the foreman said it was quite unnecessary to do so. Shortly afterwards, the jury returned a verdict of wilful murder, adding a strong recommendation to mercy.

The judge then placed upon Gregson's head the piece of cloth known as the 'black cap', and told him, 'The sentence I am about to pass upon you is a sentence in which I have no discretion. If I felt that I had a desire to pass upon you a lighter sentence I would have no power to do so. The law has decreed that when a man is found guilty of murder, the only sentence that can be passed by a judge is death,' He continued, 'I have no more doubt it is a case of murder than I have of my own existence.'

Although Gregson had been recommended to mercy by the trial jury and a memorial from the citizens of Wigan had been despatched, Home Secretary Bruce found himself 'unable to find sufficient grounds to justify any interference with the due course of law'. Gregson would be hanged.

The execution at Kirkdale was fixed for Monday 10th January 1870 at 8 am. Executions had until then taken place publicly on Saturdays at noon, but were since held on the third Monday morning after the judges of assize had left the town.

Gregson's execution was the first at Kirkdale under the Private Executions Act of 1868. Apart from the hoisting of a black flag on the prison tower, there would be nothing to indicate to the people outside that a hanging had taken place. Press reporters were allowed to view the execution, but their number was strictly limited.

On New Year's Eve 1869, eleven days before he was due to be hanged, Gregson sent the following letter to his family from the condemned cell:

> My Dear Parents, Brothers and Sisters, I should like very much to see you all once more. This last meeting, my Dear Mother, on earth is the only trouble I now have, for all my hopes of Heaven rest on the promise made to sinners – that through the merits of Jesus Christ, God will take me to Himself. That promise it is that enables me to look forward to a happy deliverance beyond the grave. My faith is strong in the goodness of God, and I hope to die a sincere Christian. Hoping, Dear Mother, you will forgive me all my wickedness to you, as I hope and trust my Heavenly Father will forgive me all my offences against Him, and trusting we all may meet in Heaven, I remain, your affectionate and truly repentant son, John Gregson.

The actual execution process, as witnessed by a reporter, was described thus:

> The culprit looked ghastly pale. The blanched cheeks, the sunken eyes, the quivering frame, all proved the mental anguish the unfortunate wretch was suffering. Having reached the treacherous platform, the poor fellow, whose arms were pinioned in the usual manner, cast a fearful look at the fateful beam. The comparative composure which he had maintained up to that time seemed utterly to forsake him. His lips moved as if repeating the portentous words of the solemn service. When the rope was round his neck be was heard to utter again and again the words 'Lord Jesus, receive my soul'. The executioner (Calcraft) quickly placed his victim in the required position on the drop, drew a white cap over his features, and then, with a cruel mockery of friendship, shook the culprit's hand. He stepped behind and drew the fatal bolt. As the drop went down with a dull heavy thud, the poor wretch was left swinging to and fro in the air. After three or four writhings of his frame, the unhappy man passed out of existence.

There were only a few spectators outside Kirkdale Prison that morning; all they witnessed was the raising of the black flag. This was in sharp contrast to the thousands of people that used to gather for the previous open-air public spectacles. Six policemen stood on duty outside the prison gate, but they had nothing to do.

A second letter was written by Gregson, and was dictated by him on Saturday 8th January. The letter ended like this:

> I also beg of you to avoid bad company, drunkenness and Sabbath-breaking, for if you could only see and feel the benefit of placing your trust in God, instead of thinking so much of this world, you would feel as happy I feel. Give my kind love to the children, and let them be brought up in the fear of the Lord. Accept the same yourselves, and believe me to be your affectionate but unfortunate son.

A Strange Blow

Richard Spencer was a fishmonger and poulterer who had a shop at 287 Breck Road in the Anfield district of Liverpool. In 1872 he was sixty years old. Fifteen years previously, his wife left him and he began living with a 16-year-old girl called Lizzie, with whom he had been ever since. When Spencer's business folded, they went to live together in Gregson Street, Everton. The events of the night of 8th August 1872 led to Spencer being indicted for her murder.

That night, Spencer and Lizzie, both being sober, went to bed as usual. At about 7 am the next morning, Lizzie was awakened by what she described as 'a sharp blow' to the side of her head.

'What have you been doing, Richard?' She asked him.

'I want us to die together,' he replied.

Panic-stricken, Lizzie ran to a neighbour's house some distance away. It was clear that she had been wounded in some way and was bleeding from the head. The neighbour went straight over to Spencer's house and into his bedroom. She found him bleeding from a wound in the forehead and from another on the side of the head, behind one of his ears. Baffled, she asked Spencer: 'What have you been doing to Lizzie?'

He replied: 'I want to see her. Send her to me.'

Lizzie went back to see him.

'Kiss me and forgive me for what I have done,' he said to her. She complied, but asked him again what he had been doing in order to injure her. At this, Spencer produced a revolver.

Spencer had shot Lizzie without her realising it – one of the chambers of the gun had been fired at her. A further two rounds had been fired by Spencer at himself in an attempted suicide.

They were both taken to the Royal Infirmary, where, after three days, Lizzie Wharton was pronounced dead. Spencer recovered and was released from hospital on 26th September. On her deathbed, Lizzie swore that she had never been unfaithful to him. She said that he was suffering from what she called 'the horrors' of alcoholism. He became convinced that someone would attack him when he was asleep and to protect himself, the deluded Spencer would sleep with a knife under his pillow. He had often threatened to kill Lizzie and then commit suicide; now he had only carried out part of his threat. Lizzie had paid the penalty.

On 16th December, when Spencer was brought to trial before Mr Justice Mellor and a jury for the murder of Lizzie Wharton, he looked like a feeble old man. His head was bandaged and he sat throughout the whole of the trial with his head resting on the dock bar. He looked like a broken man.

There was no doubt that Spencer had taken Lizzie's life, but the question was raised of whether he was insane at the time of her murder. Defence counsel Thurlow put it to the jury that Spencer's mind had been affected by the loss of his fishmongers business. He said that it was possible he had been trying to shoot himself when one of the rounds accidentally struck the unfortunate Lizzie. After all, claimed Thurlow, there was no reasonable motive for why he should deliberately shoot her.

Mr Justice Mellor, in his summing up, said: 'Nothing is more difficult to ascertain than the motives which direct human actions'. The judge also told the jury: 'Nothing is more dangerous than to be led away by ingenious speculations upon the necessity of a motive'. Richard Spencer was found guilty of murder and sentenced to death.

The execution, provisionally fixed for Monday 6th January 1873, was postponed until the 8th because hangman Calcraft had another engagement. The delay gave Spencer false hope of a reprieve.

On the Monday morning, Kirkdale's protestant chaplain, Reverend Pigott, tried to get Spencer to confess to the crime. However, Spencer said: 'I have no recollection whatsoever of having done the deed for which I am to die. If I did do it, I must have been out of my senses. I know I have brought the poor woman to ruin, but I have no recollection. I loved her too dearly. She has been the cause, through her misconduct, of bringing me to ruin.'

Pigott told reporters that Spencer was 'more resigned to his fate' than any other person he had seen in similar circumstances. As for Spencer, on the morning of his execution, he said: 'I do not wish to live, but spare me this terrible death, although I am ready to die.'

He was pinioned in the chaplain's room and led out a few hundred yards to the gallows. Meanwhile, the chaplain intoned the litany for the dying as the church bell rang out a funeral knell. The morning was so dark that the doomed man would not have seen the gallows until he was a few yards from it. Until the drop fell, Spencer repeated the words: 'Almighty Lord God and Jesus Christ, forgive me my sins and receive my soul'.

Spencer had a mercifully easy death. Not a muscle of his body was seen to move as it hung on the rope. It was later said that those who were most accustomed to these 'ghastly sights' affirmed that they had never seen anyone die more easily or so instantaneously upon the gallows.

Incidentally, it seems that Richard Spencer was born in gaol. His father was also said to have been hanged for murder.

Poorly Executed

On Monday 11th August 1873, a woman called Ellen Shears – the wife of a ship's steward – was at the Cambridge Music Hall in Liverpool's Mill Street, when she was approached by 25-year-old James Connor and asked if he could buy her a drink of wine. Mrs Shears refused his offer. Shortly before 11 pm, Ellen left the hall and was standing on the corner of Jackson Street. Connor came up to Mrs Shears and accused her of stealing some money from him.

'You are very much mistaken', she said to him. Upon that, without any argument or comment, Connor struck the woman with several violent blows, either with his open hand, or with his closed fist. She collapsed on the pavement. Two men passing by on the opposite side of the street came over, and one of them, James Gaffney, asked Connor why he had hit her. Without uttering a single word in reply, Connor drew a clasp knife from his pocket and stabbed Gaffney in the neck.

The knife had just missed Gaffney's jugular vein, but he instantly fell to the ground, bleeding profusely. Whilst he lay on the ground, Connor struck him again with the knife.

Gaffney passed away the following morning, aged forty.

Gaffney's companion, a man named Metcalf, managed to knock Connor down, but he got to his feet, retrieved the knife from the floor and ran after Metcalf, whom he then tried to stab. Luckily, the knife slashed his clothes, but did not manage to penetrate Metcalf's body.

Connor was later arrested and, on 18th August, was put on trial for murder at the Summer Assizes.

After Mr Foard had presented the prosecution's case, defence barrister Bernard, contended that Gaffney had provoked Connor into stabbing him, and consequently his client was guilty only of manslaughter. Mr Bernard told the jury: 'There is a want of evidence to show that there had been any malice aforethought in Connor's mind'.

Summing up, Mr Justice Brett told the jury that unless they believed that Gaffney had provoked Connor to such an extent that the crime could be reduced to manslaughter, they must return a murder verdict.

After a fifteen minute absence, the jury handed the judge a question in writing. They wanted to know if a verdict of manslaughter would be justified if Connor thought that Gaffney was about to strike him; his lordship agreed. However, after another half hour, the jury returned to court again. The foreman declared: 'My lord, we are unable to agree on a verdict'.

This time, Mr Justice Brett told them, in no uncertain terms: 'It is your bounden duty to agree a verdict. If you do not, you will have to stay until you do agree.' After a further absence of one and a half hours, the jury, at long last, made up its mind. Connor was guilty as charged.

After placing the black cap upon his head, Brett said to Connor:

The jury has found you guilty of having slain a man with a deadly weapon without any provocation whatever. You have cruelly abused a defenceless woman, and when a man, doing simply what was his duty as a citizen, spoke to you and endeavoured by mere speech to interfere, you, with a cruel and cowardly brutality – a brutality which has become the crying vine of this country – at once drew a knife and struck him a deadly blow. Not content with one blow, you were about again to strike the man when he was on the ground. Immediately afterwards, you struck another man with the same deadly weapon. It was nothing but the mercy of providence that saved the man's life. You have been found guilty of a wicked, cruel, cowardly, and unpardonable crime, and you must meet your fate. I tell you honestly and fairly that I can see no mitigating circumstances in your case, and no hope of mercy for you.

Brett then pronounced a sentence of death. While the judge was speaking to him, Connor declared, 'If I hear any more of this it will only make me laugh'.

His execution, on 8th September, was a complete disaster. When Calcraft released the trapdoor, Connor descended with a great thud, accompanied by the crashing sound of timbers giving way. The rope had broken. Connor, who had plummeted down, leaned precariously against the woodwork at his side. Moaning and groaning, he was heard to cry out: 'Oh dear! Oh dear!' As warders lifted him up, Connor, in great pain, asked Calcraft: 'What do you call this? Do you call this murder? Surely, this is enough? I stood it like a brick the first time. I think you should let me off now!'

Connor was put in a chair while a fresh, thicker rope was obtained. By now, he was trembling violently. During a delay of eight minutes, Father Bonte prayed with Connor, who repeated: 'Jesus have mercy. Have mercy upon me!' At the second time of asking, Connor had the coolness and presence of mind to adjust the white hood carefully down the side of his face. One reporter wrote: 'There were some vibrations of the body, some convulsive shivers, a brief struggle in which the hands were clenched tightly, then it was all over'.

Fit of Rage

On 1st November 1873, a group of people was living in a lodging house at 30 Chisenhale Street in Liverpool. Together with Thomas Corrigan there were his parents and his sister, a man called Canavan, the Harris family, and a woman called Martha Knight with whom the young Corrigan, a labourer, was cohabiting. Corrigan and Knight slept in a garret on the second floor; the Harrises and their children occupied a room on the first floor. Corrigan's father and mother slept in a little room on the ground floor, called the parlour. Mr Corrigan senior was the tenant of the property.

On 1st November, Thomas Corrigan came home at about 6 pm. Although he had been drinking, he was well aware of what he was doing and he and Knight went up to the garret. Old Mrs Corrigan, who was known as Mary, came in at about 6.45 pm, and Corrigan came downstairs in his stockinged feet and demanded food.

'Where is my supper?' He asked his mother.

She replied: 'It's in the oven, Tom.'

Corrigan looked in the oven but there was no supper in there. His father explained that his sister Kate had gone out to get it. Upon realising that he would have to wait for his meal, Corrigan seemed to take leave of his senses. He grabbed his mother by the shoulders and then struck her a blow in the face. Then he threw her to the floor, screaming out: 'Give me sixpence!' Like a wild animal, he began attacking everyone in the room. First, he charged at his father, who immediately beat a hasty retreat. Then he got hold of Mr Harris, but then apologised, before grabbing Canavan by the hair, and pulling him to the floor. When Canavan got back on his feet, Corrigan knocked him down again, shouting: 'I'll clear the bloody house!'

Canavan fled, and after locking the front and back doors behind him, Corrigan turned his aggression upon his unfortunate mother. Firstly, he opened the front of her dress and searched her for money, without success. Then he took hold of her by the hair, raised her to a sitting position, and flung her on to the floor again.

The situation then worsened. Corrigan got hold of a table for support and began jumping up and down on his mother's body, between her stomach and her chest. It was as if he were dancing a jig on her inert form. After a short time, Mary Corrigan's eyes closed and she appeared to be lifeless.

Next, Corrigan vented his anger at his partner Martha Knight. After knocking a panel out of the parlour door, he shouted upstairs to her: 'You come down!' At the third time of calling, Martha came downstairs. Corrigan told her to get him a candle, and as she was by the fire lighting it, he punched her three times in her ribs.

'Get me water, you bitch!' He screamed. She brought him a mug of water and he promptly threw it over his mother's face before proceeding to wash it with a wet sponge. Mrs Corrigan was revived by the water and pleaded with her son: 'Thomas, don't, you are a good son, Thomas, don't.'

Mrs Harris and Martha managed to undress Mary and put her into a bed in the parlour. Meanwhile, Corrigan continued his tirade, shouting at his mother: 'Give me money, you bitch! I know you have money!'

Somehow or other, Mary managed to drag herself upstairs on her own. After beating Martha with a leather belt, Corrigan discovered that his mother had left the parlour and was outraged. He ran upstairs and screamed: 'Go down, you drunken bitch!'

The already dreadful situation then deteriorated even further. Corrigan took hold of his mother and threw her naked body down the stairs. He ran down after her and began to thrash her with the buckle of his belt, around her head, face and ears.

'Mrs Harris! Mrs Harris!' She screamed, bleeding from her face and nose. She then proceeded to have the life beaten out of her. Corrigan did another bizarre stamping jig on her body, of which Mrs Harris later said: 'He danced upon her from the crown of her head to her abdomen'. Then, sickeningly, Corrigan took a knife from the kitchen table and, holding the blade to his mother's neck, snarled: 'I may as well hang for this bitch as anyone else.' Mrs Harris, on her knees, begged Corrigan not to kill Mary. She said: 'For the honour of the great God, don't use the knife on your mother!'

Mercifully, Corrigan threw the knife sway. Martha screamed in terror, whereupon he punched her in the face. Martha and Mrs Harris tried to lift Mary from the floor, but to no avail. Corrigan refused to help, saying: 'She's only gammoning. I won't put my hand to the drunken bitch'.

Eventually, he calmed down a little and threw his dying mother on to a bed. A rattle from her throat indicated that perhaps her dreadful suffering was at last at an end.

'She's not dead yet, Mrs Harris', said Corrigan. He then proceeded to wash his mother's body all over with a sponge. 'Do you think she is dead, Mrs Harris?' He asked.

'Feel her pulse, Thomas', she replied.

'She's all right', said Corrigan.

Mrs Harris put a mirror to Mary's mouth. It misted over; amazingly, she was still alive. Having sent Martha out for some whisky, Corrigan poured some down his mother's throat. 'It went down as if into an empty barrel', said Mrs Harris later. Martha brought another tot of whisky and Corrigan once again poured it down Mary's throat and down her nose.

Minutes later, Mary Corrigan passed away.

'Thomas, your mother is dead', announced Mrs Harris.

'Give me my boots. I will leave the house.' He replied. Realising the enormity of what he had done, Corrigan pleaded: 'Mrs Harris, you must all save me. Say she was drunk and fighting, and fell in the street.'

When Corrigan's father got back home, a crowd of people – attracted by curiosity – entered number 30. Father Ross, a Catholic priest, went in too.

'Violence has been used to this woman. Who has done it?' He demanded. Shamefully, Corrigan, his father, and his sister Kate all told Ross that Mrs Corrigan had been drunk and had fallen in the street. The priest took one look at her body and realised her family was not telling the truth; it was clear from the state she was in that she had been brutally beaten to death. Corrigan fled, but was arrested by Constable McDowell at 9.30 pm in Chisenhale Street, only fifty yards or so from the house. Corrigan said to the officer: 'Get a doctor for my mother. She has died suddenly.'

When he was charged with murder at the Central Police Office, he replied: 'You are wrong.'

Predictably, a matricide case created great public interest both locally and nationally. On Tuesday 16th December 1873, a huge crowd assembled outside St George's Hall, many of whom had no chance of getting into the public gallery; they simply hoped to get an idea of what was going on from people coming out of the court early.

The judge of assize that day was Mr Justice Quain. The main witness for the prosecution was Mrs Mary Harris. She gave a detailed account of the events at 30 Chisenhale Street on that November evening. Dr Donovan, surgeon at the Northern Dispensary in Vauxhall Road, described Mary Corrigan's dreadful wounds. As well as severe head injuries, she had sustained three broken ribs. Her face was badly swollen, and her left eyeball was ruptured and hung outside its socket. When Donovan first examined the body, blood was still seeping from the mouth, nose and left ear. As a result of a post mortem two days later, Donovan testified that death was either caused by a skull fracture and a resultant brain haemorrhage, or from a fatal injury to the abdomen. Both causes of death were feasible, said the doctor.

Before the case for the prosecution was closed by Crown counsel Williams, a statement by Corrigan was read out by the Clerk of the Court. Corrigan had said: 'On Saturday evening my mother and I had been drinking. After that I went to bed, and I can't remember anything'.

It was fairly clear that Corrigan had committed murder. Unless he was found to be insane, his days were numbered. Mr Thurlow, who had been appointed by the judge to defend Corrigan, put forward to the jury the old chestnut of temporary insanity caused by drink. He quoted from a legal book, which said: 'Drunkenness is often material where there is a question as to the intent with which an act is done.' Thurlow argued: 'The very fact that the prisoner has killed his mother shows that at the time be was not in a state to know what he was doing. Corrigan was labouring under some terrible and sudden fit of "the horrors".'

The defence counsel put to the jury that Corrigan was 'labouring under some terrible internal disorder of the mind'.

'There was not that intent', said Thurlow, 'that must be an ingredient in murder'. Summing up, Mr Justice Quain shot down Thurlow's defence. The judge told the jury: 'There is no ground whatever that would justify you in returning a verdict of manslaughter. Your verdict must be one of murder, or acquit the prisoner on the ground of insanity'. His lordship then explained for the jury the law as it concerned drunkenness. He said: 'With respect to a person *non compos mentis* from drunkenness, a species of madness, it is a settled rule of law that if the drunkenness be voluntary, it cannot excuse a man from the commission of any crime, but on the contrary, it must be considered as an aggravation of what he does amiss.'

After only a ten minute delay, the jury convicted Corrigan of murder. He received an automatic death sentence from Quain.

By the time of the execution on 5th January, several innovations had come into operation at Kirkdale Prison. The condemned criminal no longer had to walk some hundred yards or more to the scaffold. An area called 'the reception room' had an exit door within a few feet of the stairs leading up to the scaffold. The hangman – a newcomer to Liverpool who went by the pseudonym of 'Anderson' – had also dispensed with Calcraft's long-standing habit of shaking hands with the prisoner on the scaffold.

Following the drop, Corrigan's hands were seen to clasp convulsively. A half-smothered cry of 'Oh' was heard from beneath the white hood. His body shivered and quivered for several minutes on the rope, and after five minutes, it was motionless, except from swaying in the morning breeze.

The body was laid to rest in the prison yard shortly after noon, in a plain deal coffin, painted black. After the execution, a plaster cast of Corrigan's head was taken, in order to be studied according to the now outmoded practice called phrenology – the examination of a person's skull shape in order to assess character.

False Accusation

In 1874, Henry Flanagan was employed as a shoemaker in his aunt's shop at 7 Bent Street, off Scotland Road. Flanagan's aunt was Mary Flanagan, a 53-year-old widow. Although Mary was a very fat lady, she was in excellent health. Other shoemakers and their wives were lodging at number 7; their names were Flynn, Meehan and Ryan. On the evening of Saturday 4th April, when their week's work was over, the men bought several quarts of beer, and quite soon the shoemakers, including Henry Flanagan, were under its influence.

At about 8.30 pm that evening, one of Flanagan's married sisters came into the house. Quite by accident, she bumped against Flanagan, and a pair of boots, belonging to Mary, fell from underneath his arm. Immediately, Mary accused her nephew of stealing the boots, thinking that he intended to pawn them to pay for more drink.

At this accusation, Flanagan lost his temper.

'I will have a life before morning'. He spat.

Realising that the drinking session had been spoiled by Flanagan's attitude, Flynn, Meehan and Ryan went off to their beds. However, Flanagan, despite a good deal of persuasion, refused to turn in, and a result, he and his aunt Mary were left alone in the kitchen.

At about 4 am the next morning, Mrs Ryan went downstairs to light the fire, looked into the living room and saw Henry Flanagan lying asleep on a mattress. Mary was lying on the floor on the other side of the room. Later that morning, Ryan and Meehan went downstairs on their way to a public house and noticed Mary was still lying on the floor. They touched her, and realised that she was dead. Flanagan did not waste much time in clearing off from Bent Street. He asked for his awl and hammer and said: 'I am going to Manchester to look for work.'

He fled with a man called Edward Neill who was also a shoemaker that worked for Daniel Flanagan, one of Mary's sons. On the morning of the 5th, the two men went to a shop in Fontenoy Street. Here, the assistant, Mary Kavanagh, remembered selling Flanagan two hats at a shilling each and two coats at 1s. 6d. each; he had given her a sovereign for some change. Flanagan asked Neill to go with him to Manchester, saying that he had plenty of money and telling him, 'I will give you a good spree'. The previous night he had had no money at all. Now he seemed to be rolling in cash.

At McGee's confectioners in Great Crosshall Street, Flanagan and Neill bought two bottles of apple wine. Both men offered assistant Margaret Aikin a sovereign, but she did not have the change and asked them if they had anything smaller. They said they did not but promptly drank the wine anyway, promising they would call again to pay, which they never did. They both went to Lime Street station, where Flanagan found out that there would be no train to Manchester until 2.30 pm because it was a Sunday. Flanagan told Neill: 'I must get out of town before that', so the two men began walking towards Prescot. On the way, Flanagan changed another sovereign at a tobacconist's and told Neill to keep the change, as he had plenty of money. Further on he changed another sovereign. When Neill asked him how he had got so much money, Flanagan said: 'George, I'll tell you the truth. My aunt was drunk on Saturday night. I took a purse out of her breast and took the money, and put the purse back again. She was alive then'. Neill commented: 'It was a wonder the old woman let you take the money off her when she was drunk. She was harder about money when she was drunk than when she was sober.' Flanagan explained that he had had 'a little bit of a tussle' with his aunt and that he tried to violate her.

On reaching Prescot, they both had a drink in a pub and Flanagan told Neill that he wanted to go to Glasgow. Flanagan said he was going to Rainhill to catch a Glasgow train and they went their separate ways. At about 9.30 pm that night, a policeman called James Swarbrick found Flanagan lying on a footpath at Knotty Ash. Swarbrick recognised Flanagan as fitting the description of the wanted man; it appeared as if he had been making his way back to Liverpool. When asked by the policeman, he gave his correct name.

'Do you know anyone in Liverpool?' asked Swarbrick.

'No, not a soul', Flanagan replied.

When questioned further, Flanagan claimed he had walked to Manchester and back, and that he was 'dying of hunger'. Swarbrick was far from satisfied and took the fugitive to Knotty Ash police station.

There, Flanagan was charged with his aunt's murder. In reply to the charge, he said: 'It can't be helped now.'

On the morning of Friday 14th August, Henry Flanagan appeared for trial at St George's Hall. The trial was to cover two whole days – an unusually long time for those days.

Dr McConnell acted for the Crown and Dr Commins for the defence. The final witness for the prosecution was medical man Dr Cormack. He was called to 7 Bent Street on Sunday morning, 5th April. By that time, Flanagan had vanished with Neill on his travels through West Lancashire. The doctor had found Mary lying on her back on the floor, near the fireplace. There were red patches on the face, neck and part of the shoulders that were speckled with small black spots. The whites of the eyes were bloodshot and the pupils dilated. The jaw was locked tight, and the teeth were stuck fast in the tongue, which protruded. The doctor said that these symptoms indicated sudden death from either strangulation or suffocation, probably the latter. In cross-examination by Dr Commins, Dr Cormack discounted apoplexy as the cause of death.

In his address to the jury, defence barrister Commins stated that there was 'a total absence of motive'. The money that Flanagan took, said Commins, might have belonged to him and not to his aunt, and that someone else in the house could have killed her. Commins said that it was in his client's favour that he had remained at Bent Street for over two hours after his aunt's death, and had even left his coat and boots at the scene of the crime.

Dr Commins claimed that death by suffocation, 'was not a certainty', and Mrs Flanagan could have died of apoplexy. He suggested that Flanagan did not flee from Liverpool *because* he had committed murder, but because his cousin Daniel Flanagan, accusing him of murder, had threatened to kill him. Finally, Commins advised the jury: 'Give the prisoner the benefit of any doubt that may arise in your minds.'

Summing up, Mr Justice Archibald described the case as circumstantial, because no-one saw Flanagan attack his aunt. He told the jury that it should have a degree of proof 'as would lead you to convictions and conclusions which, in any serious affair of ordinary life, you would be disposed as reasonable men to arrive at.' The judge told the jury that it had to decide whether a murder or a natural death had occurred; if they believed that Mrs Flanagan was suffocated, who was responsible? They had to consider whether the allegation that Daniel had accused Flanagan of murder and threatened to kill him, was true.

His lordship, like hundreds of judges over the years, deplored the evils of drink. He said: 'I hope that the time will come when we shall get rid of that terrible curse and plague of the country. If that vice were removed, I think I am speaking within bounds when I say that one-half, or at least more then one-third, of the persons who stand in the dock would not stand there.'

The jury took only five minutes to find Henry Flanagan guilty. When be was brought back up into the dock, he walked 'steadily, with a most unconcerned air' to the bar. After being sentenced to death, he put his folded arms on the iron railing in front of the dock and asked: 'Can't I speak, my lord?' Warders on each side of him shook their heads but be cried out: 'I did not intend to cause her death!'

As Flanagan was being taken from the dock, an elderly man reached over and shook his hand. It was later rumoured that this man was Flanagan's father. Henry Flanagan was executed in a double hanging with Mary Williams on 31st August 1874. (see *Raleigh Street Riots*)

Raleigh Street Riots

On 20th April 1874 there was an outbreak of fighting amongst a large group of women in Raleigh Street, Bootle. It lasted for several hours and resulted in a number of broken windows. Most of the women involved were worse for wear through drink, and the cause of the riotous dispute was ill-feeling between Mary Williams, who lived at 60 Raleigh Street, and the two sisters of Nicholas Manning, who lived at number 50. Although Manning had nothing to do with the quarrel, he was later to pay a heavy price for the part his sisters played in the local disturbance.

Several hours after the dispute had subsided, at about 8.30 pm, Manning was walking home along Raleigh Street when without any provocation at all, Mary Williams, who was standing at her doorway, hurled a small basin at him. It struck him a painful blow on the head. Undeterred by this incident, Manning passed by and went into his house.

About ten minutes later, Manning came back in the opposite direction and had to pass Mary's door for a second time. Just then, Mary drew a pistol out of her apron pocket and shot Manning in the right shoulder, causing him to collapse in a heap on the pavement. A passerby heard Manning cry out: 'I am done for!', to which Williams was alleged to have replied: 'Yes, and there are two or three more I will do it to before the night is over.' Manning was taken to the Bootle Borough Hospital, where he died on 3rd May.

On the same night as the shooting, Williams was arrested and charged with attempted murder. Referring to the incident she said, 'no, not to murder him, I only did it to frighten him'. When she was arrested, she declared: 'It is alright, it is me that done it, and I would do it again.' On the way to the police station, she was alleged to have told the police officer: 'I did it, and no-one else is to blame but me. It was me that shot him, and it is an honour to my country.' A search of her house revealed nine slugs, a box of caps, a ramrod, two powder flasks and a pistol, loaded with a slug and capped ready to be fired.

After being committed for jury trial at the Liverpool Summer Assizes, Williams said: 'I am innocent. It was my husband that did it.' At her trial, Dr Willes, house surgeon at Bootle hospital, testified that the immediate cause of Manning's death was blood poisoning. In cross-examination by defender Foard, Dr Willes said: 'Some members of the medical profession believe that blood poisoning is more frequent in hospitals than other places, but that is simply due to overcrowding.' At the post mortem, a lead ball was found in the body.

Mr Foard contended that there was no intent on Williams' part of doing any grievous harm to her victim. However, during Foard's speech to the jury, he was interrupted by Mr Justice Archibald. The judge commented that the question was whether or not Williams fired the pistol intentionally. If she did, the law assumed that there was malice aforethought in her mind. Continuing his speech, Mr Foard said: 'It is perfectly reasonable to believe that Williams fired the pistol with the simple purpose of frightening Manning, who had given her great provocation. There was no evidence', he said, 'to show by whom the pistol had been loaded, or that Williams, when she fired it, knew that it was loaded'.

In his summary, Judge Archibald told the jury:

> If you believe that the prisoner fired the pistol with the intention of shooting at the deceased and of wounding him, and that death resulted, she will be guilty of murder. If, on the other hand, she fired it carelessly and negligently to frighten him, without any intention of doing him harm, it will be manslaughter.

The jury quickly found Mary Williams guilty and she was sentenced to death. She fainted and had to be supported by a female warder as she was removed from the dock.

The double hanging of Henry Flanagan and Mary Williams took place at Kirkdale on 31st August 1814; they were both executed at 8 am that morning.

Alderman Geves, the Mayor of Bootle, had tried to get Williams' sentence commuted to imprisonment for life. Colonel Brace, the Chief Constable of Lancashire, sent a glowing report of Mary's character to the Home Secretary and Williams continued to claim that it was her husband who had fired the fatal shot. He had subsequently disappeared and the police were searching for him. It was suggested that Mary admitted the crime to allow Williams to escape, in the belief that her innocence would later be proved.

Mary was deserted by her father when she was twelve and her mother had died some years earlier. She had had very little schooling. Her husband used to beat her regularly and often left her for long periods of time; on many occasions she had been compelled to take refuge in the workhouse.

On the morning of her execution, as she was climbing to the 'reception room' next to the scaffold, Mary turned to the reporters and said in a firm voice: 'Upon my conscience, gentlemen, it was my husband fired the pistol'.

Marwood, from Hardcastle in Lincolnshire, was the executioner that day. His ropes were thinner than the ones Calcraft had used, but were made of jute, so they were softer and stronger, and had a greater breaking strain. Whilst having her legs strapped together, Williams, prompted by Father Bonte, recited the Lord's Prayer, the Hail Mary, and the Apostles' Creed. She then shook hands with a female warder and said the words 'Goodbye, God bless you all.' When Marwood removed the bolt of the trapdoor, Williams and Flanagan fell side by side.

About four seconds later, the legs of both victims were seen to twitch, but their struggles were brief and their deaths were both swift.

It was many years since a woman had been hanged in Liverpool. In 1843 the notorious Betty Eccles was despatched for poisoning several of her family members in order to get money from a burial society.

Mary Williams, 30, left many children. The eldest child, a girl of twelve, was placed into the Industrial School, adjacent to the prison. Her infant child, and several others, were sent to Walton workhouse; a few more were cared for by relatives.

Terrible Trio

On Monday 3rd August 1874, a man was cruelly attacked and robbed in the centre of Liverpool. Three young men were held responsible. They were Peter Campbell, 17, a carter; John McCrave, 20, a labourer and Michael Mullen, 19, a dock porter. The attack occurred at about 9 pm at the corner of Tithebarn Street and Lower Milk Street. The three men were known as 'corner men' and their aim was to extort money from passersby by fair means or foul. On this occasion, their scheme failed. All three were arrested and put on trial for murder at the Winter Assizes of 1874, before Mr Justice Mellor and a jury.

The victim, Richard Morgan, was 25. He worked as a porter in a provisions warehouse and had been married to his wife Alice for thirteen months, after an eight-month courtship. On Monday 3rd August, Richard and Alice had travelled over the Mersey to spend time at New Ferry Gardens. On their return to the Liverpool landing stage at about 8.30 pm, the couple was met by Richard's brother Samuel. They all walked from the stage up Chapel Street, where they called in at a public house. Richard had two pennyworth of whisky in ginger beer; Alice and Samuel both had a glass of ale.

When they left the pub, the trio walked up Tithebarn Street, heading for the Morgans' home in Leeds Street. At the corner of Lower Milk Street they noticed a group of young men standing outside a pub.

As Richard approached, one of the youths, later identified as John McCrave, said menacingly: 'Give us sixpence to make up the money for a quart of beer!' As he did so, McCrave took hold of Morgan's hand.

'What do you work at?' Morgan asked, squaring up to him.

'We work at knocking down such men as you, to take it off you if we can.'

Fearful for her husband's safety, Alice pleaded: 'Don't knock him down.' 'It's a good job you have got a woman with you,' one of the men said. Seconds later, McCrave punched Morgan. The blow struck him behind the left ear and knocked him on to the pavement. McCrave then whistled to Mullen and Campbell who came over and began to kick Morgan. Their attack was so vicious, that Morgan was propelled across the street, a distance of some ten yards.

Alice Morgan threw herself across her husband's body in an attempt to protect him, but Campbell dragged her away and kicked her too. Campbell then fell on Richard and put his hands round his throat to throttle him, whilst kicks rained upon Morgan from the three assailants. Although Richard's brother Samuel succeeded in flooring two of them, he could not prevent their eventual escape. Not one person in a crowd of onlookers did anything to help.

The attackers took to their heels, as Samuel chased them down Lower Milk Street and into Vauxhall Road. He laid into Mullen, telling him that he had murdered his brother. They all managed to escape, but as Samuel made his way back to Tithebarn Street, he found the three men standing in the street. They ran away from him again; their courage had apparently now deserted them.

Samuel managed to catch up with McCrave and grabbed hold of him, whereupon the latter drew a knife. A man from the mob came up behind Samuel and put his knee in the small of his back, thus forcing him to let go of McCrave, who fled once more. Samuel continued his pursuit, but eventually lost sight of his target, in Pownall Square; several women on the corner of a side street had deliberately blocked his way.

It became clear that the cowardly assailants of Richard Morgan were not brave when they were on their own. That very night, Samuel found McCrave standing on a pub corner, captured him, and handed him over to the police.

During his pursuit of the offenders, Samuel had been backed up by a picture-frame maker called Lipson, who had been present when McCrave had pulled a knife on him. Together, they pointed McCrave out to a policeman called Adam Green. At first, Constable Green had said that he was attending a fire and could not help because he had a special duty to perform. He was watching over a store of cotton that had been fire-damaged, and was told by his Inspector not to leave the cotton until all was quiet. At about 9.30 pm, Green was told by two women that a man was getting kicked in Tithebarn Street. He went there and found Richard Morgan lying on some steps outside McFie's bonded sugar warehouse; from there, four men carried Morgan to the

Northern Dispensary. Green later took Morgan's dead body home to number 10 Court, Leeds Street.

Green eventually arrested McCrave. On the way to the bridewell, he charged him with having killed Morgan. In reply to the charge, McCrave said: 'I know nothing at all about it, but if he is dead it will be murder.' McCrave was very drunk when he was arrested.

The next morning, McCrave was formally charged by Detective Officer William Hale.

'It was not me that kicked him', he said to Hale. 'I was fighting with the other man. Mullen and Campbell were fighting with him when I came up, and I was drunk at the time.'

With McCrave safely in custody, it was now vital to track down Mullen and Campbell. On the morning of 14th August, a river police officer, Constable Ben Whittle, boarded the ship *J.C. Robinson* on the Mersey. Three stowaways were handed over to Whittle, one of whom was Michael Mullen. He was taken to the police hut on the dockside, where he gave his name as 'William Murphy'. Later, Mullen was identified by Alice Morgan at the police office.

'Not me.' Mullen replied when he was charged.

A month later, on 13th September, acting on information received, Detective Hale went to number 4 House, 3 Court, Gascoyne Street. In the middle room of the house there was a man lying on a bed. Noticing something bulky under the bed, Hale stooped and pulled out the hapless Peter Campbell. To a murder charge, Campbell was alleged to have said: 'I was there at the time, but I was not near the man. It was Mullen and McCrave who were fighting with him.'

At their trial on Monday 14th December, the three prisoners were charged with the murder of Richard Morgan. Because the attack was a joint venture, it did not matter who dealt Morgan the actual fatal blow. All three, in law, were equally culpable and were therefore tried together.

Medical testimony was provided by three doctors, one of whom was Dr George Cascaddan, house surgeon at the Northern Dispensary. He was the first to examine Morgan, who had been dead on arrival. Amazingly, Cascaddan said that he could find no sign of violence inflicted on Morgan's body that night. It was only when, two days later, an autopsy was carried out with Dr Cribb and Dr Brady, that bruises were detected on Morgan's left arm and on his left side. Yet another examination was then carried out, this time in the presence of doctors Taylor and Cavanagh. Death was at last attributed to 'shock to the system following excessive violence'. Although Morgan had an enlarged heart with considerable fatty deposits, this condition was judged not to have contributed to his death.

In court, a 16-year-old youth called William Alston testified that he knew the three accused men. McCrave was known locally as 'Holy Fly'. Alston had seen all three kicking Morgan.

Evidence from a boy called Bernard McCarthy provided light relief for those on the public benches, but it must have caused Dr Commins M.P., McCrave's counsel, a degree of exasperation. Cross-examining McCarthy, he asked the boy: 'Can you tell me where any kick struck him?'

'Oh, that won't do. How could it strike him?' The boy replied.

'Come, come, you need not be saucy', said Commins. 'You have come here to speak the truth?'

'Yes', replied the boy, 'I came here to speak the truth, but not to be puzzled out of it'.

Dr Commins put the question to him again: 'Where did any kick strike him?' To this, the boy replied pedantically: 'How can a kick strike him? They did not strike him, they kicked him'.

The case against Campbell was insubstantial. Mr Cottingham, speaking for him, submitted that his client's case 'differed materially from that of the other two prisoners'. Two prosecution witnesses had failed to identify him, so Campbell could not, claimed Cottingham, be held responsible for the acts of the other two men. In cross–examination, Detective Officer Hale had said that he knew nothing against Campbell.

Dr Commins, for McCrave, said: 'Killing in hot blood in a sudden affray is not murder.' Mr Shee pointed out that Mullen did not supply the death blow and should, he said, be acquitted.

Mr Justice Mellor told the jury that it would not be wise for them to decide that the three prisoners had a common intent to rob or to obtain money by threats and violence.

'If you find this way', said the judge, 'all are guilty of murder. The evidence is scarcely sufficient to warrant you in taking that view.' The judge continued: 'However, if you were to find that the three had the common design of assaulting people, it would not make much difference who struck the first blow'.

Finally, his lordship deplored the inaction of spectators in not helping to apprehend the culprits and, in one instance, holding Samuel Morgan back.

The jury retired at 7.30 pm to consider its verdict. At 8 pm the jury returned to say that it found all three prisoners guilty of wilful murder. There was a recommendation to mercy for Campbell.

Mr Justice Mellor then pronounced sentence of death. Describing the appearance of the three murderers, one reporter wrote: 'Mere striplings they were, all about the same height, each with narrow shoulders and a drooping head, characteristic of their class.'

As he left the dock, Mullen, who was weeping, shouted to his brother: 'Come down, Tom, and see me!' Campbell called out to the judge: 'Can I see my mother?' McCrave said to someone in the packed court: 'Goodbye, old boy!'

Campbell was reprieved two days before he was due to be hanged. McCrave and Mullen were executed with William Worthington on 4th January 1875. (see *Water-Gypsy*)

Water-Gypsy

The 1870s were busy years for the Leeds and Liverpool Canal. Heavy and bulky goods could be carried safely and cheaply on water. Coal was brought into Liverpool from the Wigan district, as well as from small pits along the way. Imported goods were transported in the opposite direction. The horse-drawn flat-bottomed barges were known locally as 'flats' and the men in charge of these vessels were called 'flatmen'. Many of the flatmen lived almost permanently on board their boats, often with a wife and several children. For years, these canal people were often referred to as 'water-gypsies', and their cosy and colourful craft formed a characteristic part of the Victorian country scenery.

William Worthington was a flatman. He lived with his second wife Ann and his step-daughter Mary Prescot on board a boat called *Ada*. When their boat was moored in Liverpool, they used to stable their horse in a yard at the back of Vauxhall Road.

On the night of 29th August 1874, Susannah Daly, the wife of John Daly, a carter, was at home with her husband at 327 Vauxhall Road. At about 11.30 pm she heard a woman screaming outside. The screams continued for the best part of fifteen minutes. On her way to bed, Mrs Daly opened a rear window and looked out, and in the yard, she could see a woman in a stooping position. A man was standing over the woman and was kicking her. Mrs Daly recognised the man as William Worthington. She shouted out to him: 'Are you going to murder the woman? I'll send for a policeman if you carry on kicking her!'

When Worthington continued his attack, Mrs Daly closed her window and went outside. She opened her front door and could hear a man speaking to Worthington. It was John Kerr, a next-door neighbour from number 325.

'What have you been doing to the woman?' Mr Kerr asked.

'What business is that of yours?' replied Worthington.

Kerr then blew a whistle to summon a policeman and Constable James Flint soon arrived on the scene.

Unfortunately, Flint refused to take Worthington in charge, saying that the couple should settle their quarrel back at their boat. Incensed at the officer's attitude, Mrs Daly said to him: 'We might as well have no protection in this town'. By now, Ann Worthingon's face was covered in blood.

'Just look at the woman's face!' Mrs Daly said to Flint.

'It's not my face, it's my ribs!' Ann replied in despair.

'Won't you give him in charge?' Kerr asked Ann, to which she replied: 'Yes, take him.' Nevertheless, Flint walked away. The Worthingtons returned to their boat. It was now about midnight.

The step-daughter Mary, who was Ann's child, was on board when William and Ann arrived at the boat. As soon as William got into the cabin he resumed his attack on her. He gave her one kick in the abdomen, with such force that it broke the bone of her stays and knocked her off her seat on to the cabin floor. She put her head on her bed and lay that way all night, with her body on the floor. Without undressing, Worthington lay on the floor and fell into a drunken stupor.

The next morning, Worthington promptly started the day by kicking Ann again. He then hit her over the head with a poker.

'Oh Ann', he said mockingly, 'have I hurt thee?' before leaving the boat.

Later that morning of the 30th, Ann Worthington received a visit from a friend – Margaret Sutcliffe of Bennett Street, Vauxhall Road. Mrs Sutcliffe found Ann in a dreadful condition; her breathing was very laboured. It seems that Ann had been asthmatic for years and was never in the best of health.

'Ann', said Mrs Sutcliffe, 'I think you are in bother again'.

'Yes', replied Ann weakly.

Later that week, Worthington gave Ann five pounds to pay for a doctor, but she told him she would get one when she got to her sister's house in Wigan. The delay in getting medical aid was a very serious mistake on her part. She did not arrive at her sister's house until 5th September, a full week after being injured.

Ann arrived at her sister – Catherine's – in a cab. She could hardly walk and so Catherine called in Dr Stewart right away. On 9th September, Worthington came to see his wife. He was obviously the worse for wear for drink, and he said to her: 'Ann, how art thou?' Far from pleased, Ann replied: 'Get away from me! Thou hast kilt me!' Catherine told

Worthington to clear off. 'We do not want drunken people here while we are reading prayers', she said.

Ann passed away on Thursday 10th September. On the same day, Worthington was arrested at Ince by Constable Leyland of the Wigan police. Leyland then handed him over to Detective Officer Thomas Grubb, who charged him with murder. To the charge, Worthington replied: 'It is a bad job. I wouldn't it had happened for a thousand pounds.'

After appearing before the magistrates and being committed for trial at the Liverpool Winter Assizes, Worthington came up at St George's Hall on 16th December before Mr Justice Mellor. Mr Samuel and Mr Shee appeared for the Crown. The defence counsel was Mr Cottingham.

During the presentation of the prosecution case, William Roocroft, a Wigan surgeon, testified that there was an old collarbone fracture, together with fresh fractures of two of Mrs Worthington's ribs. The immediate cause of death was attributed to 'pleuro-pneumonia'.

As mentioned earlier, Constable James Flint failed to arrest Worthington when he was called to the scene of his initial kicking attack. Mr Justice Mellor really tore a strip off Flint who, albeit indirectly, could be said to have been partially responsible for Ann's death. 'Why did you not take the man in charge?' The judge asked Flint.

'I thought it was merely a word between man and wife'. He replied. 'Is it your feeling as a police officer that whatever may be the injury a wife receives, it is not a case for police interference?' asked Mellor.

'I did not think it was as bad as it was, sir,' replied Flint.

The judge then made the following remarks, which remain equally applicable to domestic violence in the present day:

> When a policeman sees a woman with marks of ill-usage about her, and people call his attention to her, and point to the man who ill-used her, it is his duty to interfere. A man has no right to beat his wife because she is his wife. She has as much right to be protected as anybody else. The witness should understand for the future that he is bound to have a charge made if he sees the signs of recent injury. A policeman ought to interfere in such a case whether anybody interferes or not.

The judge continued: 'The mistake into which you have fallen is one into which policemen appear to fall in districts where disturbances are frequent. Slight disturbances between husband and wife ought not to be meddled with, but where there are marks of violence, policemen ought to act at once. If you had taken the prisoner in charge that night, he could not have gone with his wife to the boat, and she might have been alive now. You had better remember what you ought to do in future.'

'I will sir,' replied Flint.

In his closing speech to the jury, Mr Cottingham submitted that the crime, if murder at all, was what he called 'constructive murder', that is to say it was a case of 'a man inflicting unlawful injuries on another, but not intending at the time to cause death.'

Cottingham said that the jury 'should consider the condition of life to which the prisoner and the deceased belonged.' According to Cottingham, the fact that Worthington 'had not entertained any felonious intent' was proved by 'his anxiety that the deceased should have proper medical assistance.' In all probability, claimed Cottingham, Mrs Worthington would have survived had she called in a doctor immediately.

The judge, addressing the jury, said that he could see 'no ground for a reduction to manslaughter', he said: 'it does not seem that you can draw any other inference but that the prisoner is guilty of murder'.

The jury took fifty minutes to agree with the judge, but recommended Worthington strongly to mercy. Before sentencing Worthington to death, the judge said to him: 'I beseech you not to buoy yourself up with any false hope or delusion, but to prepare as if for death, for it is in the highest degree uncertain that the recommendation of the jury will have any effect. I beseech you therefore ... to endeavour to obtain that pardon at the throne of grace which the human law denies you.'

A triple execution, of William Worthington, John McCrave and Michael Mullen was carried out at Kirkdale at 8 am on Monday 4th January 1875. At that hour in midwinter, only a few streaks of dawn were visible. The morning was foggy and raw. The three criminals were Roman Catholics, but none of them had ever been instructed in religion, nor had they ever attended a church service. McCrave and Mullen were resigned to their fate. In contrast, the ex-flatman Worthington thought he ought not to be hanged. He said he never intended to kill his wife.

The condemned men rose at 5.30 am. At 7 am Father Bonte said Mass in the chapel and they received communion. Although McCrave and Mullen ate very little for breakfast, Worthington tucked into a hearty meal.

A flight of steps led up to the small room behind the scaffold. Before Worthington was placed over the drop, Mullen and McCrave shook hands with him and then embraced each other. All three men prayed on the scaffold, repeating in unison the litany said by the priest: 'Lord be merciful to me, a sinner', and 'Lord Jesus, have mercy upon me'. The other two men were then brought out in turn and before launching them into oblivion, hangman Anderson shook hands with the three men as they stood under the beam. The bolt was withdrawn. Although the victims fell only about three feet, the drop was sufficient to produce a comparatively painless death. This was indicated by the bodies scarcely moving after the trapdoor had fallen.

Collision Course

In July 1875, William Baker, aged 35, was the manager of a Liverpool public house called The Rainbow, situated on the corner of Basnett Street and Houghton Street in Williamson Square. Baker's victim was 34-year-old Charlie Langan, an ex-cab driver who was living on his wits and on his winnings from backing horses and running an unofficial bookmaking service. Neither Baker nor Langan were what the Victorians would call respectable men.

William Baker despised the Langan family and their associates. In May 1875, John Holmes, a stableman from St Andrew Street, was standing at the Williamson Square cab stand. In a conversation with Baker, Holmes said: 'I am going to settle the Langans. I've got a toy in my pocket that's going to fix them good and proper.'

Baker and Langan were on a collision course that came to fruition on the night of Friday 9th July, in Seymour Street, off London Road. On that night, Baker started drinking at Mills' public house on the corner of Hopwood Street and Scotland Road. He was in company with three other men – Hartley, Stannard and Parkes. At about 11.00 p.m., the four men set out to make their way back towards Baker's Rainbow Inn. However, they were not destined to reach it that night.

Baker and his men called in several pubs and drank ginger beer, locally called 'spruce'. Meanwhile, Langan was drinking in an illegal 'blacking shop' run by a Mrs Partridge. The shop was at a house in Back Bridport Street, on the east side of London Road, directly behind the Alexandra Theatre.

When Baker and his three companions knocked on the door, Mrs Partridge refused to let them in.

'You can't come in here, it is bent', she said, so they were forced to go on their way.

A few minutes later, at about 12.30 am, Langan left the blacking shop in the company of Edward Taylor, Anthony Curran, and a man called Phillips. They went to the top of Back Bridport Street, heading to the

Swan Inn, and as they crossed over to St Vincent Street, they saw Baker and his three men standing opposite the Swan.

As they were passing, Baker called out: 'Charlie, I want to speak to you'. The men carried on walking so Baker shouted again: 'It's you that I want, you sneaking sod.'

Near Judge's boot shop, Curran decided to stand between Baker and Langan, acting as a peacemaker.

'For God's sake, Billy', he said. 'Don't have a quarrel here, let him be until tomorrow.' At that point, however, Baker took a revolver out of his pocket, stretched out his hand towards Langan and shot him in the head. Langan dropped to the pavement.

'For God's sake, get a four-wheeler! The man is either dying or he's dead!' Curran screamed. He bent down to Langan who was lying motionless on the floor: 'Charlie, speak to me!' He pleaded, but there was no reply. Curran went with Langan in a cab to the Royal Infirmary in Pembroke Place. Langan was dead on arrival.

Immediately after the shot had been fired, a policeman had arrived on the scene. He asked Edward Taylor if Langan had killed himself.

'No, officer,' Taylor replied, pointing at Baker. 'That is the man who shot him. You will find a pistol in his pocket.'

Baker was taken into custody, and sure enough, in his right-hand trouser pocket, there was a five-barrelled revolver. One barrel had been discharged and the remains of a cartridge were inside it. Baker insisted that he had not meant to hit Langan with the pistol but that it had discharged accidentally.

Henry Taylor, a Liverpool Corporation watchman, was on duty in London Road, when the incident occurred. He stated that he was about five feet away from Baker when he saw him put the pistol directly to Langan's head and fire the weapon.

Baker came to trial on 17th August before Mr Justice Archibald. Mr McConnell and Mr Segar prosecuted and Mr Pope Q.C. and Dr Commins acted for Baker. He appeared in court dressed in a close-fitting shooting jacket with a white handkerchief showing in his left breast pocket.

After Mr McConnell had outlined the facts of the case and called witnesses to the shooting, Mr Hall, resident medical officer at the Royal Infirmary, described the condition of Langan's body when it was brought to him at about 1 am on 10th July. Hall found a small bullet wound towards the back of the skull, behind the left ear. The hair around the wound was singed, showing how close the weapon had been to Langan's head when it was fired. On removing the scalp, Hall discovered that the bullet had perforated the bone, entered the brain, and struck the inside of the skull, fracturing the temporal bone. The bullet had been removed from Langan's brain and was produced in court.

The jury had to decide whether or not Baker's claim that the gun had fired accidentally was true. It seemed from the evidence of various eye-witnesses that Baker had deliberately aimed the weapon at Langan's head. However, when addressing the jury on behalf of Baker, defence counsel Pope told the jury to consider that Baker may have intended to strike Langan with the pistol, whereupon it may have accidentally gone off. In this case, Baker would be found guilty of manslaughter. Mr Pope said: 'If there was such a verdict in the English Law as 'Guilty, with extenuating circumstances', it would apply here.' Baker, who was a little man, was dealing, said Pope, with 'a set of well-known and well-recog-nised ruffians as ever disgraced the streets of Liverpool'.

Mr Pope asked the jury to take a merciful view of Baker's position. Showing the pistol to the jury, he said: 'This gun is an instrument of imperfect construction. It is probably out of order, and if it cannot be cocked now, is it not reasonable to suppose that the lock is so imperfect that the smallest amount of concussion, when the blow was struck, would cause the hammer to fall and produce the explosion?' Finally, he added: 'The prisoner's life is all I ask, and it is for only that that I plead to you.'

Summing up, Mr Justice Archibald warned the jury not to take the easy way out and convict Baker of manslaughter. He told the jury:

> If you believe it was an accident, you must not allow yourselves to resort to an alternative of that kind, unless on the whole, you are perfectly satisfied in your judgement that there is ground for it, because it would be a most flagrant miscarriage of justice if men on their oaths, who are bound to decide the case according to the evidence, would – simply because an alternative of manslaughter is put before them – adopt that, instead of employing their minds in the fair and proper investigation of the evidence.

The judge made his opinion crystal clear by saying: 'No provocation by words, no insults, no blow even, can justify a man in discharging a deadly instrument like that, instantly at his assailant. Carriage of a pistol is evidence of malice, and no jury ought to endeavour to escape from returning a verdict of wilful murder.'

Surprisingly, the jury took an hour and a half to return its guilty verdict, giving Baker a strong recommendation to mercy. Before being sentenced, Baker used his opportunity to speak:

I have very little to say. I think if my counsel had taken a different course, a verdict would have been awarded otherwise. I am not blaming my counsel, but I think he took the wrong course in my defence ... Had the minds of the jury been reached with reference to this man and his threats towards me latterly. I think also it might have extenuated my case.

Finally, Baker tried to portray himself in a good light: 'I have been in fear, and have been a martyr since I have been under my father through their threats. It appears from the judgement that has been passed upon me, that I am still a martyr'.

While the jury was out, a reporter painted a vignette of the crowded court:

The crowd in the court began to laugh and talk together as unconcernedly as if they were whiling away the time between the acts of a play at the theatre. The ladies, almost exhausted by the oppressive heat, vigorously fanned themselves. A general hubbub of rustling of dresses and free conversation ensued, which was only put to an end by the reappearance of the jury.

Whilst in his cell, Baker submitted a petition – forwarded to London by Mr Blackhurst, his solicitor – in which he described how the bad feeling between the two groups of men had arisen. He said that he had known Langan through his betting connections, which he had given up when he got married and became the manager of his father's pub, The Rainbow, in Basnett Street.

After he repeatedly refused to serve drink to Langan and his brothers, they began to harass and threaten him, in one instance with a deadly weapon. Baker said his only temporary relief from living everyday in fear, was when Langan was imprisoned for a garrotte robbery. He told the police, that because of this continuing worry for his own safety, he had bought a revolver to frighten Langan and his friends, as he was too afraid to go out alone. His reprieve was not successful. After his spell in the condemned cell, Baker was a broken man. On the morning of the execution he was very weak and had to be given brandy.

William Baker was hanged with Edward Cooper on 6th September 1875. (see *Murder at Sea*)

Murder at Sea

On 23rd January 1875, a British ship, the *Coldbeck*, left Liverpool for Valparaiso, Chile. Before the vessel reached its destination, while travelling on the Pacific side of Cape Horn, a tragedy occurred on board. As a result, Edward Cooper, an able seaman, was brought back to Liverpool in irons to face a murder charge at St George's Hall in August of that year, before Mr Justice Archibald at the Summer Assizes.

On 20th April, Thomas Gibson, a sailmaker on board the *Coldbeck*, was in the ship's sailroom when Cooper and another seaman came in, followed soon afterwards by the boatswain, Edward Jones. Gibson heard Jones say something to Cooper in a sharp tone. Jones and Cooper, between whom no love was lost at the best of times, exchanged some angry words.

Cooper then told Gibson he was going into the forecastle and would be back in a few minutes. When he returned, he placed the barrel of a revolver against Gibson's head. Alarmed, Gibson told Cooper: 'Mind what you're after with that thing.' He then asked him if he could have a look at the firearm and Cooper handed it over.

'It's fully loaded, you know.' Gibson told him.

'Yes, I know it is', Cooper replied, and put the weapon into his pocket. Gibson remembered that he had seen a similar weapon in the sea-chest of a seaman by the name of George Murray.

Two days later, on 24th April, shortly after 5 pm, Cooper and several other seamen were having tea in the forecastle. Jones, who was standing in for the second mate, entered the room.

'Cooper, come and help us haul in the middle staysail'. Cooper, without replying, stayed where he was, so Jones repeated his request and added:

'I cannot do all the work myself.' Jones left, and when he realised that Cooper had once again ignored him, he sang out sarcastically: 'Cooper, where are you?'

'I am having my tea'. Cooper snapped.

'It is time enough for your tea when I have mine', said Jones angrily. At this remark, Cooper simply began laughing at him, and it was clear from the atmosphere in the room that the situation was about to get out of hand. Jones then swore at Cooper and snarled: 'You have had your way long enough! He continued, 'You have been blowing about the deck long enough. Come here now and fight it out like a man.' No fight erupted, but Cooper went away and returned with the revolver in his hand.

Jones, by now a frightened man, told Cooper to put the weapon away, but to no avail. Beside himself with anger, Cooper screamed twice to him: 'I will shoot you! I will shoot you!' before stretching out his arm and discharging the revolver at Jones' chest.

Jones fell to the floor on his left side, his hands over his chest. There was a cut on his cheek that seemed to have been caused when he fell to the deck. He looked up and murmured: 'May the Lord have mercy on my soul. I am done for'.

Another seaman, Emile Samuelson, managed to lift Jones up and walk him as far as the main hatch, before he fell to the floor. He was then carried into the cabin where his clothes were torn open, revealing a bullet wound under his left shoulder. He died shortly afterwards.

After firing the shot, Cooper went to sit in front of the fire in the forecastle. When questioned about what he had done, he said that Jones had cut him with a sheath knife, and that he had shot Jones in self-defence. Although Cooper did have a cut on his thumb, no-one had seen Jones with a knife, nor was a knife found after Jones' death.

When the captain of the *Coldbeck* charged Cooper with murdering the boatswain, he replied: 'Yes, I knew it would happen as soon as he was put in charge.' Cooper was then chained up in irons. The next day, Jones' body was cast into the Pacific in a ceremonial burial at sea.

On the ship's arrival at Valparaiso, the various witnesses to the tragedy were examined before the British Consul. Cooper did not sail back to Liverpool on the *Coldbeck*, but was shipped home on board the steamship *Iberia*. On arrival on 23rd July 1875, Cooper was taken into custody by River Police Constable Murdoch Mackay. When charged with causing Jones' death, he simply replied: 'I have nothing to say'.

Around three weeks after his arrival at Liverpool, Edward Cooper was tried for his life at the assizes. At the closure of the case for the prosecution, Crown counsel McConnell, summarising the case against Cooper, pointed out to the jury that Cooper could not claim that Jones had ordered him to do anything that could be described as an unjustifiable act. No knife had been seen, even though Cooper's thumb had been cut. A prosecution witness had testified that although Jones was in the habit of carrying a small pocket knife, he was never seen with anything as dangerous as a sheath knife.

In his address to the jury, defence counsel Potter deplored Jones' action in challenging Cooper to a fight. Potter said: 'It is not by asking a seaman to come out and fight it out that discipline on board a ship is likely to be maintained'. Citing provocation, Potter asked the jury for a manslaughter verdict. He said: 'Had not sufficient injury been inflicted on the prisoner to make him think that he was in peril of life or limb at the moment he fired the pistol?'

After the judge had summed up, the jury retired at 3.30 pm. At 5 pm, after thinking long and hard about Cooper's culpability, it returned, and its foreman handed a slip of paper to Mr Justice Archibald. Exactly what was written on this paper was not revealed, but the judge told the jury: 'All I have to say in answer to that is that whatever you desire to say should come in a regular way from all of you, but I see no objection to any of you stating what you wish. You had better consider whether you are all agreed on that point.'

After a few moments of consultation, the jury gave a verdict of 'guilty of wilful murder, with a strong recommendation to mercy'. Cooper was then given the automatic sentence of death.

Edward Cooper and William Baker were hanged simultaneously at Kirkdale on Monday 6th September 1875. Cooper had also submitted a petition to the Home Secretary, Mr Cross, but like Baker, was not reprieved.

Cooper's reprieve petition was prepared by ship-owners Nicholson & Sons and signed by a thousand seamen. It was forwarded to the Home Office by Thomas Hanmer, the secretary of the Liverpool Sailors' Home.

When Baker and Cooper were being pinioned by Marwood in the reception room, they said to each other: 'God bless you'.

Baker was helped up the stairs on to the scaffold by Chaplain Pigott. While the ropes were being adjusted, Cooper called out in a loud voice: 'Gentlemen, goodbye all. May the Lord have mercy upon me. Goodbye

Father Bonte'. He then turned his head in the direction of the five reporters and said to them: 'All I have to say, gentlemen, is that I did not get justice'. Baker simply said: 'Lord have mercy on my soul'.

While both men were quietly praying, Marwood pulled the lever to draw the bolt on the trapdoor. Neither man suffered any more; death was instantaneous.

An estimated crowd of some five hundred assembled in the brick-fields around the prison. On the roof of a house next to a tannery, some youths had clambered up in the hope of seeing inside the gaol. Stanley Road was lined with spectators and, when the black flag was raised, a rush was made for the prison wall. A long line of men, women and children put their ears against it, trying to hear the sound of the drop, but by then the men had fallen and were already lifeless.

Before the two bodies were buried, a well-known phrenologist, Mr Bridges of Mount Pleasant, was allowed to take plaster casts of the two criminals' heads. After due consideration, Mr Bridges announced that Cooper seemed to have been a murderer on impulse. As for Baker, Bridges could find nothing good in his character.

Newspaper Parcels

The murder of 7-year-old Emily Mary Holland by William Fish at Blackburn in 1876, remains to this day one of the most dreadful and ghastly crimes ever committed in Great Britain. The case, tried at Liverpool in July of that year, created an immense interest throughout the length and breadth of the country. This interest was augmented by the publication of the committal proceedings, which in those days involved the presentation of the prosecution case before the actual trial.

On the opening day of the trial, vast crowds besieged St George's Hall and filled the building to bursting point. Reporters from virtually every newspaper in the country attended, but many of them were unable to hear anything at all. Some pressmen were ejected by other enthusiasts trying to squeeze into the packed courtroom, and women were excluded as the evidence was deemed to be too upsetting.

Fish was once described by the *Liverpool Daily Post* correspondent: 'He wore a seedy black suit and displayed at intervals a dazed and stupefied expression. The noticeably protruding forehead and the great size of his head, as contrasted with his diminutive body, was even more exaggerated by the bushy appearance of his hair, which was a sandy brown. His forehead so protruded that it was impossible from any distance to see his eyes at all'.

William Fish was born in Darwen, a few miles from Blackburn. Orphaned at an early age, he was raised in the workhouse, apprenticing for a Blackburn barber. After robbing his master of a week's takings, he served a prison sentence. However, in his later years, Fish was regarded as a respectable tradesman. He kept a barber's shop in Moss Street where he worked alone, and both he and his wife were said to be members of the local body of Primitive Methodists.

Each day on her walk to St Alben's Roman Catholic School, Emily Holland had to pass Fish's shop. She lived with her parents at 110 Moss

Street, about a quarter of a mile from the school and few hundred yards from the barber's shop.

On Tuesday 28th March 1876, Emily came back home for her dinner at around 1 pm. Her mother Elizabeth gave her baked potatoes in their jackets and some fig pie. On her way back to school, Emily went to the house of her aunt, Annie Eccles, who also lived in Moss Street. Because it was examination day at the school, Emily was wearing her Sunday clothes – a black coburg frock and a lilac pinafore, with a leather belt.

Emily's cousin, 12-year-old Mary Ann Eccles, saw her leaving school at 4.15 pm. At 4.30 pm, she also saw Emily at the side of Cox's tobacconist shop with three halfpence in her hand. Freddie Cox, the shopkeeper's son, remembered her coming in and buying half an ounce of smoking tobacco. However, Emily was not buying tobacco for her father; she was running an errand for William Fish.

Emily's father, James Holland, worked as a mechanic in a cotton mill. When he got home that day at 5.40 pm he discovered that his daughter had not returned from school, so he went to search for her. After having no luck in finding her, he told the police that Emily had gone missing.

Two days later, on 30th March, Mrs Alice White of 73 Bastwell Terrace noticed a parcel lying in the field at the back of her house. She unwrapped the newspaper parcel and discovered to her horror that it contained the body of a little girl with its head and legs dismembered.

On the same day, a farm labourer, Richard Fairclough, found a similar newspaper parcel in a drain at Lower Cunliffe. This one contained a pair of legs. Significantly, both parcels had been wrapped using newspaper sheets from the *Preston Herald*.

When the body parts were examined, samples of short hair of various colours were found on them; not only head hair, but also from beard trimmings. This immediately made the police question where such hair had come from and led them to visit the barber's shop operated by William Fish.

In the shop they found many back copies of the *Preston Herald*, some of which they believed had been used to wrap up the body parts. A few weeks later a bloodhound was taken into the shop and in an upper room, the dog showed a great interest in the fireplace. Up the chimney police found parts of a small charred skull and some other bones. Under a pile of coal beneath the stairs they also found part of Emily Holland's dress. Fish was immediately placed under arrest and put in front of the magistrates. In the meantime, the Blackburn police released a man called Taylor, upon whom suspicion had at first fallen.

On the day after his arrest, Fish made a complete confession in a signed dictated statement to the police:

> I told Constable William Parkinson that I had burnt part of the clothes, and put the other part under the coals in my shop, and now I wish to say that I am guilty of the murder. I further wish to say that I do not want the innocent to suffer. At a few minutes after five o'clock in the evening I was standing at my shop door in Moss Street when the deceased child came past. She was going up Moss Street. I asked her to bring me one half-ounce of tobacco from Cox's shop. She went and brought it to me. I asked her to go upstairs, and she did. I went up with her. I tried to abuse her, and she was nearly dead. I then cut her throat with razor. This was in the front room near the fire. I then carried the body into the shop, cut off the head, arms and legs, wrapped up the body in newspapers on the floor, wrapped up the legs also in newspapers, and put these parcels into a box in the back kitchen. The arms and the head I put in the fire. On the Wednesday afternoon I took the parcel containing the legs to Lower Cunliffe, and at nine o' clock that night I took the parcel containing the body to a field at Bastwell, and threw it over a wall. On Friday afternoon I burnt part of the clothing. On the Wednesday morning I took part of the head which was unburnt and put it up the chimney in the front bedroom. I further wish to say that I did it all myself. No other person had anything to do with it.
>
> The foregoing statement has been read over to me and is correct. It is my voluntary statement, and before I made it I was told that it would be taken down in writing and given in evidence against me.
>
> (Signed) William Fish

At Fish's trial, the Crown was represented by two Queen's counsel– Mr Higgin and Mr Pope. At the end of his opening twenty-minute speech, Mr Higgin told the jury that he intended to call witnesses to prove that Fish's confession was true. The trial itself was virtually a foregone conclusion. The only real point at issue was whether or not Fish was insane at the time he committed the crime. With this object in view, Fish pleaded not guilty to the murder charge.

After the other prosecution witnesses had given their evidence and after Fish's statement bad been read out, Dr William Martland, surgeon to the Blackburn police and senior surgeon at the East Lancashire

Infirmary, gave the forensic evidence. The child, said Martland, had suffered unspeakable violence, been sexually assaulted and had eventually died from having her throat cut.

Mr Blair, who had been directed by Mr Justice Lindley to defend Fish, addressed the jury. Blair said he could not disguise from himself the difficulty with which he had to contend. The jury was probably by then reeling from the plethora of forensic detail. Probably the greatest sensation was caused when a prosecution witness called Peter Taylor lifted up a wooden box with an inner glass casket, and produced from it, one by one, pieces of bone, then fragments of a dress, and finally a skull, with long golden hair clinging to it.

Blair, describing Fish, said: 'The poor remnant of humanity that is in the dock is at this moment a focus of horror to the whole of England.' Going for an insanity verdict, Blair said: 'The poor creature at the bar, when he perpetrated the act which he undoubtedly committed, was not a person thoroughly responsible for his actions. The prisoner had not shown one particle of ingenuity or cleverness in the means he took to remove the traces of the crime. The body parts were thrown where they would not long remain concealed, the trunk thrown uncovered into a field.'

In his peroration, Blair said: 'This crime transcends in its hideous circumstances all that you have ever read or heard of. Can you believe that any sane man after having committed an act of that kind, could the same evening shave or cut the hair of a customer? If you find a verdict against the prisoner, you will have to say, beyond the possibility of reasonable doubt, that he is not insane.'

Blair's plea to the jury was all very well, but he must have known that he had called no defence evidence to indicate that Fish was insane. There was no evidence of insanity in the family, or from anyone who had observed Fish, either in a consulting room, or while awaiting his trial in Kirkdale.

The judge told the jury that if it believed Fish's confession to be true, there could be no question that he was guilty as charged. He said: 'You would not be justified in finding any man insane unless there was evidence to prove the insanity. It cannot be inferred that his hideous and wicked act was accounted for on the ground of insanity. There was not a particle of evidence presented to support the defence counsel's plea, except the hideousness of the crime itself.'

The jury took only a few seconds to make up its mind. Each juror simply nodded to the foreman, who stood up and announced Fish guilty. Before being sentenced, Fish said: 'My lord and gentlemen of the jury, at the time I did the deed I did not know what I was doing. It came over me all at once. I never had such a thought in my head when I sent for the 'bacca.'

As sentence of death was being pronounced by Mr Justice Lindley, Fish swayed backwards and forwards, clutching on for dear life to the rails of the dock. In a faint, with a wild expression of terror in his eyes, he was carried down the steps by two burly warders.

William Fish was hanged alongside Richard Thompson on 14th August 1876. (See *Friend or Foe*)

Friend or Foe

In the spring of 1876, Richard Thompson was living with his parents at 119 Haigh Street in the Everton district of Liverpool. Thompson used to work away at sea, but of late he had been earning money as a plasterer's labourer. He had never been in trouble with the law and was considered to be of good character.

Thompson was friendly with a man named William Corfield who lodged with the Thompson family. The two men shared a bed, a common arrangement in the overcrowded conditions of Victorian Liverpool.

Corfield had a young sister called Mary. She lived in a house in Coronation Street with a young couple called Margaret Jane and John Henry Blundell. Thompson, who was very fond of Mary, used to visit her regularly at the Blundells' house. However, after some time, Blundell told Thompson that he objected to his being alone with Mary in the house. Normally, Thompson and Blundell were the best of friends and Thompson had even been best man at Blundell's marriage to Margaret Jane in December 1875. However, because Thompson ignored numerous warnings to do his courting elsewhere, Blundell ordered him out of the house. This action generated considerable ill-feeling on Thompson's part, against his erstwhile good friend.

On 8th April 1876, whilst they were in bed, Thompson told Corfield about his dispute with Blundell and how he would 'have it out' with him one day soon.

Thompson's anger towards Blundell did not dissipate, but instead grew more intense. On Friday 14th April, Thompson, when passing Blundell's house, saw Mrs Blundell sitting on her doorstep. Shaking his belt at her, he shouted: 'Send your husband out, and I will put him in his coffin before the night is through!'

The following night in Coronation Street, a young man called John Richard Crowe came upon Thompson, who was singing the chorus of a song and appeared to be drunk. Crowe noticed that he was carrying an open knife in his hand, and when Thompson began waving it in the air, he asked Crowe: 'How would you like that up you?'

'I would not like it at all'. Crowe replied.

'It is not for you. It is for some of them up there.' Thompson then continued to stagger onwards to his destination.

That evening, Blundell and Corfield had left Blundell's house to help in the removal of some furniture for a friend. At about 11 pm, the two men, each carrying a box on his shoulder, were walking along Coronation Street when they met Thompson.

'Here's Dick'. Corfield said to Thomspon, at which Thompson then drew his hat forward on his head and made as if to button his coat; his attitude was uncannily threatening.

'What's to do with you, Dick? What are you on for?' Blundell asked him, in a friendly tone, devoid of anger or hostility.

At that point, Thompson put his hand in his right pocket, drew out his open knife and caught hold of Blundell by the left arm. He struck him savagely with the blade, about a dozen times in his left arm, side and chest.

Blundell dropped the box he was holding and shouted out in terror: 'I have been stabbed!' As Thompson was about to stab Blundell yet again, Corfield jumped on to him and received a cut on his neck, before Thompson ran away into the night.

Hearing screams, police constable 305, in Haigh Street, ran to the scene. Blundell was bleeding profusely, but amazingly was still alive, and was rushed to the Workhouse Hospital in a cab. Unfortunately, one of the knife-thrusts had punctured one of his lungs and he died the following Monday evening, 17th April.

After leaving Blundell wounded in the hospital, Corfield and the police constable went to Thompson's house in Haigh Street. Thompson was standing in the doorway, but when the officer approached him, he slammed the door shut and bolted it. After a few minutes of trying, the officer managed to break down the door and searched inside for Thompson, who had already made his escape.

Only hours later, on the Sunday evening, Thompson gave himself up to P.C. 108. He told the officer: 'I could not walk the streets for people shouting at me what I had done.'

The post mortem on Blundell's body was carried out by Dr Irving of the Workhouse Hospital. There were three very deep wounds on the arm, one of which was four inches long. On the left side of the chest there was a one-inch wound that had cut through the sixth rib and penetrated the lung about an inch deep. Other wounds were present in the back and in the left buttock. Blundell's death was attributed to haemorrhage, chiefly from the wound which had pierced the lung.

Richard Thompson was tried at the assizes before Mr Justice Lindley and a jury on Saturday 29th July, the day following the conviction and condemnation to death of William Fish for the Blackburn murder.

The major issue at this trial was whether or not Thompson had been provoked by Blundell and had then stabbed him in a scuffle. Apart from Corfield, the only other person called by the prosecution who saw anything of what happened was a woman called Emily Heel who lived in Stitt Street. Emily said she heard a scream and, on turning round, saw Thompson and Blundell fighting. She then saw Thompson stab Blundell several times.

'You have a knife!' She cried, rushing towards him.

'I have not,' Thompson screamed, pushing her away.

At the trial, defence counsel Shee said that there was 'sufficient evidence of provocation to reduce the crime to manslaughter'. He submitted that Blundell had challenged Thompson to a fight, blows were exchanged, and then Thompson had used the knife.

Speaking to the jury, Mr Justice Lindley was clear and succinct when he said: 'If stabs were given with the intention of inflicting serious injury, and death ensued, the crime would still be murder, unless it could be reduced to manslaughter by an amount of provocation.'

The jury was out for only ten minutes. There was no recommendation to mercy for Thompson. Asked if he had anything to say, Thompson replied:

'I would have liked to have seen my witnesses. He threatened to lay me out.' After being sentenced and taken from the dock, Thompson cried bitter tears.

Thompson was hanged with William Fish at Kirkdale on Monday 14th August 1876. Both prisoners left cautionary messages for the other prisoners at Kirkdale. Fish's message said:

> You can see by my bad end through breaking off Sunday School and through bad companions ... After I neglected it, I went from bad to worse. It is not too late for you to mend. If I had served God instead

of Satan I should not have been here. Avoid those bad cheap journals on which I wasted so much spare time. May we meet in heaven, through God's mercy.

Thompson dictated the following:

... they must attend their places of worship regularly and avoid drunkenness and keep from bad company. The first person who ever took me into a public house and gave me a glass of beer was the first witness who was called against me at my trial. I used to be dead against the beer.

Marwood officiated, and the executions went carried out without a hitch. At 8 am a crowd of some three hundred stood outside the gaol. One scribe wrote of Thompson: 'A finer built fellow never suffered death at the hands of the public executioner.'

Bad to Worse

At around 10 pm on Monday 16th July 1877, John Golding went to the house of his neighbour, Daniel Lloyd, who lived at 5 Derby Place, in Liverpool's Edge Hill district. Golding and Lloyd were on bad terms at the time, and things were soon to get worse between them.

When Golding knocked on Lloyd's door, it was answered by Lloyd's wife Sarah. Golding asked her if her husband were at home as he wanted to speak to him. Sarah admitted her husband was in, but told Lloyd to leave and shut the door in his face. To say that Golding was less than pleased by this rebuff would be putting it mildly; he was incensed.

About twenty minutes later, Golding called on another neighbour, bricklayer Thomas Vaughan, to ask for his help in teaching Lloyd a lesson.

'Come, Tom', said Golding, 'let's soften Lloyd's head'.

Vaughan refused. He thought that Golding, who normally was a quiet, peaceable and well-behaved man, was acting completely out of character.

Coincidentally, Sarah Lloyd also went round to see Vaughan, at which point Golding called her vile names and then threw his cap at her for good measure. After Sarah went home and told her husband how she had been insulted by Golding, he went out looking for him and found him in the street, speaking to a woman called Mrs Bowness.

'Do you want to fight?' Lloyd asked bluntly, and before waiting for a reply, Lloyd struck Golding on the head and then returned home. Mrs Bowness persuaded Golding to go to back his own house and she went with him.

When they got inside Golding's house, he would not be placated. He put his hand up to his injured head.

'Must I lose my blood and have nothing for it?' He asked, before grabbing hold of a poker and rushing out of the cellar in which he lived.

Soon afterwards, while she was sitting eating her supper with her husband, Mrs Lloyd heard a pane of glass shatter in the front window of her house. As she went outside to investigate, Golding rushed past her, poker in hand, hell-bent on revenge. As Lloyd was sat at the kitchen table, Golding attacked him, raining four or five violent blows on his head with the poker. As Lloyd fell from his chair, unconscious, Golding ran away and Lloyd was taken to the Royal Infirmary with a fractured skull.

Recalling the event, his wife Sarah said: 'Blood flowed from Daniel's head as if from a pipe.' A circular piece of bone from Lloyd's head, about an inch in diameter, had cracked and been pushed down through his skull by the force of the weapon used. Although the piece of skull was removed at the Infirmary, inflammation of the brain soon set in, and on Sunday, Lloyd fell into a coma. He died on Tuesday 24th July.

In the meantime, on the morning of 17th July, Golding was arrested by Constable John Williams. Charged with assaulting Lloyd, he replied: 'He aggravated me to do it.' The offending poker, damaged and bent, was found in a cupboard in Golding's cellar.

Looking back on the events of 1877, it does appear that Golding had a good chance of convincing a jury that he was provoked into fatally attacking the unfortunate Lloyd. The difficulty that Golding's counsel, Dr Commins, faced, was that there had elapsed a considerable time interval between Lloyd's attack on Golding and the latter's revenge with the poker. Commins submitted that the killing of Lloyd was committed 'in hot blood after provocation', which implied a manslaughter rather than a murder.

The trial jury did not agree with Dr Commins, and after a short absence, it found Golding guilty of murder, with a recommendation to mercy. In 1877, the Court of Criminal Appeal had not yet been constituted. Had it been in existence at the time of Golding's conviction, the verdict might well have been reduced, on appeal, to manslaughter. As it was, John Golding was hanged with Patrick McGovern on 21st August 1877. (see *The Visit*)

The Visit

On the same day that John Golding was convicted of the murder of Daniel Lloyd, Patrick McGovern came before Mr Justice Hawkins, charged with the murder of a man called John Campbell. The swiftness of mid-Victorian justice, particularly when the evidence was direct rather than circumstantial, is illustrated by these two murder trials, both of which were completed within a day. It could be argued that, before the passage of the 1868 Act which banned public executions and the terrible disorder that they generated, both Golding and McGovern might well have been reprieved, or been convicted of the lesser charge of manslaughter. The introduction of private executions, to which the general public had no access, had markedly increased the use of the rope, not only in Liverpool but throughout the land.

John Campbell worked as a butcher. He had four children and lived with his wife and his sister, Ann Kearns, at 91 Latimer Street in Liverpool. On the night of Wednesday 18th July 1877, the Campbells had a visit from Patrick McGovern's wife. Mrs McGovern was drunk and told them that her husband had threatened her and turned her out of the house, so she stayed and ate supper with them.

At around 12.10 am she left their house with the Campbells' 12-year-old daughter, who helped her home. A few minutes after Mrs McGovern's departure, Campbell decided to go and check for himself that she had got home safely. When he got to McGovern's house, he tore a strip off him for keeping his wife out.

After a few sharp words between the two men, McGovern rushed at Campbell and stuck a table knife into his stomach, up to the hilt. He staggered home, went into his kitchen and sat down on a chair.

'Ann, I am stabbed,' he said, pointing to his side. The knife was still sticking into his body. She drew the knife out and ran to find a policeman.

After visiting Campbell and arranging his transfer to the Stanley Hospital, Constable Edward Walsh arrested McGovern, who, like his wife, was intoxicated. Campbell had been sober. He died on 24th July; a post mortem examination showed that death had occurred from septic inflammation as a result of the wounds to his stomach and liver.

A deposition was taken from Campbell's sick bed by magistrate Edward Whitely in the presence of McGovern. Campbell claimed that McGovern had rushed at him and pushed him in the chest, and even though he realised he had been stabbed, he had not seen the knife.

McGovern accused Campbell of putting his arms around his neck, which Campbell admitted to, but insisted that, 'it was only a joke.'

Dr Commins, speaking for McGovern at his trial, contended that he had been provoked by Campbell touching his wife. She had remained, said Commins, at Campbell's house until midnight, drinking, thereby fuelling McGovern's resentment of Campbell's conduct even more. Commins put it to the jury that the knife could have belonged to Campbell, who acquired the fatal wound during a scuffle with McGovern.

Summing up, Mr Justice Hawkins said there were no grounds for a manslaughter verdict. After a few minutes delay, the jury found McGovern guilty of murder.

Before being sentenced to death, McGovern said to the judge: 'I am innocent. I know nothing about it.'

'I am sorry to hear you say that you know nothing about it.' Hawkins replied.

'I don't remember, my lord', McGovern professed.

Hawkins then continued: 'The sentence which I am about to pronounce on you is not my sentence. It is the sentence of the law, which compels me to pass it'.

During the sentence, McGovern had to be kept on his feet by two warders. As he was removed from the dock, he uttered an agonised and prolonged moan.

The execution of John Golding and Patrick McGovern was carried out at Kirkdale on Tuesday 21st August 1877. This was the fourth double execution there since the passage of the Private Executions Act, in addition to a triple hanging in 1875. (see *Water-Gypsy*)

At the time, the two men were expected to be reprieved, but in hindsight, this was very unlikely. Not long before the incident with Campbell, McGovern had been released from prison after serving a term of hard labour for assaulting his wife. Furthermore, a warrant had been issued for his arrest on the charge of stabbing his brother-in-law, who had become critically ill as a result.

Heavy rain – with thunder and lightning – fell immediately before the 8 am execution. Although the two men had both been convicted on the same day, they did not meet each other until they were about to be hanged.

Golding believed his sentence to be both severe and unjust. McGovern was extremely agitated. He had to be supported when climbing the scaffold steps, and then was held on the drop by two prison officers.

'Merciful Jesus!' He called out.

Marwood had given the men unusually long drops – Golding's was eight feet and McGovern's was four feet – and the hanging did not go well. The victims 'died hard', as the saying went. McGovern's head grazed the trapdoor as it swung back into position. Each man struggled violently on the rope and died by strangulation, rather than from fractured vertebrae. McGovern's body was drawn up into a bizarre crouching position before he finally lost consciousness. The inquest jury did not see fit to criticise Marwood for any aspect of his work and he was not reprimanded for any faulty estimations of required drops.

The death sentence had been duly executed according to the letter of the law.

Drunken Dispute

James Trickett was a rat-catcher and a bird fancier, who kept a pet shop in Hopwood Street, off Scotland Road. James and his wife Mary lived above the pet shop with their two young children, and had it not been for the fact that they were both addicted to drink they might have been reasonably well-off. In the absence of drink, the couple might also have tolerated each other more, therefore avoiding their regular domestic quarrels, for which they had become well known in the neighbourhood. After years of their noisy disputes, people living near to them took little notice of disturbances coming from the Trickett pet shop. However, this was to change quite remarkably on the evening of Boxing Day, 1877.

At about 8 pm on that Wednesday evening, Margaret Brown, who lived in Great Homer Street, was walking along Hopwood Street when she heard a noise coming out of the pet shop. The shop door was closed, but the window was lit up. On looking through the window, Miss Brown, as well as hearing the cries of a woman, saw a man – presumably Trickett – kicking violently at something on the floor. After a moment, she heard the voice of a little boy: 'Mother, can't you come upstairs to bed?' Then a few seconds later, she heard the woman scream again.

Had Miss Brown been a local resident, she would have recognised the disturbance as another of James and Mary Trickett's violent disputes. She decided to go on her way, not wanting to get involved in what she probably thought was a normal quarrel between husband and wife.

About ten minutes later, two neighbours – John Shaw, a flatman who lived at 13 Hopwood Street, and Mrs Bowen, who lived at Number 1, knocked at Trickett's door. Perhaps they saw themselves as peace-makers, or more probably, they feared for Mrs Trickett's safety.

Trickett's little boy answered the door and let them in. Trickett, from the staircase, said to Shaw: 'I have killed the wife, John. Come up, Mrs

Bowen, why don't you?' Upstairs, they found Mary lying on the floor next to a knife, bleeding badly from a head wound.

Trickett started to bathe his wife's injured head with a sponge and Mrs Bowen asked him what had happened.

'Don't do me any harm, Mrs Bowen. Say she fell downstairs. Say she fell against this box', He pleaded with her.

'I cannot say that', she replied. Trickett then turned to Shaw.

'I have killed my wife.' He told him, and then asked Mrs Bowen to fetch a priest and a doctor. Instead, she found a policeman, and shortly afterwards, three officers turned up – an inspector and two constables.

When Inspector Donaldson asked Trickett what happened, he replied: 'Oh, nothing. She will soon be all right. She fell downstairs.' He added: 'My wife has been drinking for thirty-one weeks.' He explained the presence of a broken walking stick in the bedroom by saying that he had broken it across his knee some days previously.

When Dr Costine arrived, Mary was pronounced dead. Trickett said to her inert form: 'Mary, if you are dead, I suppose I will have to suffer for you.'

Charged with her murder, Trickett said to Donaldson: 'God knows I loved her. She has been drunk for thirty-one weeks'.

At that stage, he did not deny killing Mary, but on the way to the bridewell, he was reported to have said: 'It is an awful thing I am taken for tonight. I did not think it would have come to this.'

After being committed for trial from the magistrates' court, James Trickett was tried at the Winter Assizes before Baron Pollock and a jury. Dr Commins acted for the Crown, Mr Walton for Trickett.

Detailing the forensic evidence from his post mortem examination, Dr Costine said Mary Trickett had sustained several head wounds, three of which had penetrated to the skull bone. When questioned by Dr Commins, Costine said it was likely that the wounds in the head were caused by the walking stick that was found at the scene of the crime. However, he said the cause of death was an incised wound on the left breast – caused by a sharp instrument – which was about six inches deep and extended to the liver.

Defence counsel Watson had an almost impossible task to persuade the jury to return a manslaughter verdict against his client. Watson, amazingly, said that 'there was an entire absence of malice'. At the worst, he said, 'the crime was manslaughter'.

The jury retired at 4.30 pm. Ten minutes later, it returned, wanting to know if a sharp instrument had penetrated the woman's clothing. Dr Costine, recalled to the witness box, held up pieces of a dress and of a chemise, both of which were perforated and saturated with blood.

Fifteen minutes later, the jury brought in its guilty verdict, with a strong recommendation to mercy for Trickett, 'on account of the great provocation he received'.

In 1878, it was not yet possible for persons accused of a crime to give evidence in their own defence from the witness box. However, statements, read out by the prisoner from the dock, were allowed, at the discretion of the judge. Before being sentenced, Trickett was allowed to read out the following, arguably ludicrous, statement to the crowded court:

> I came home and found my wife sitting on a little stool, with her mouth, nose and arms contracted together. The front door and the stair door were open. I turned round to her and said: 'My dear, is it thus you are again? Am I never going to get any good out of you?' She made no reply. I then put some coal on the fire, and put the kettle on to make some supper. I then went into the yard for a little time. My little boy came and shouted out: 'Mammy has fallen from the stool on to the floor' When I got in I saw some caraway seeds which my wife used to eat to take away the smell of drink. I found a little bottle with about half a glass of whiskey in it. I picked it up and laid it on the parapet which went across the place where the birdcages were. I then lifted Mary from the floor, and saw some congealed blood running down from the ear by the cheek. I said to her: 'Come, old girl' so that she should not get angry.
>
> When I got her upstairs she balanced backwards, and fell with the back part of her head, as if she came on the stairs or the room door. I took her up and laid her on the bed and she swore at me. I left her there and pulled the bedroom door to. I then came downstairs and went into the cellar. I picked up a bit of wood and put it underneath the coals on the fire. I then fed the birds and smoked my pipe. A man came in and asked for two pennyworth of lark food. I then heard something upstairs. I opened the door and listened, but I heard nothing then. I went into the yard, returned, and heard something falling on the floor very heavily. I went upstairs with a candle in my hand, and I found Mary with her head against a big chest, and her body beside another chest. Seeing blood on the bed, I said: 'Oh Lord,

what is this?' I saw a bruise on her face. I burst into tears and pulled her away from the chest. I asked William Stewart to get a doctor and a policeman. When Mrs Bowen came, I took her upstairs and said to Mary: 'here is Mrs Bowen, can she do anything for you?' Mary made no reply. The walking stick had been broken since July last. I broke it across my knee when coming from the country, as my little boy knocked a birdcage off a wall with it. It was a play toy for the little boy.

Finally, starting to cry, Trickett said: 'God knows that I am innocent. I love my wife and children and I want to see the little ones. I would lay down my life for my two little boys. I see gentlemen in the court who have known me well for years. Many police officers can give me a good character.'

Passing sentence of death, Baron Pollock told Trickett that he could see no prospect of mercy, despite the jury's strong recommendation.

James Trickett was duly hanged on the morning of Tuesday 12th February 1878 at Kirkdale by Marwood. The drop was around eight feet and Trickett died without a struggle; his passing was said to have been almost instantaneous.

The Brothel

In 1879, Thomas Johnson was working as a stoker in a foundry. From time to time he lived with a 21-year-old prostitute called Eliza Patten, and in March of that year they were residing in a brothel at 59 Prince William Street, Liverpool. On the night of 21st March, the couple was thrown out of the house because Eliza was not earning enough to pay her rent. They spent the following night, a Saturday, in a lodging house.

By chance, Eliza knew Mary McCarnon, the proprietor of another brothel, at 61 Prince William Street, near to her former abode. On the morning of Sunday 23rd March, Eliza called on Mrs McCarnon and asked her if she could cook some bacon and eggs for 'Demon' – her nickname for Johnson. Mrs McCarnon said she could.

Just before noon, Johnson arrived at the house with a woman called Eliza Kelly. After Johnson had eaten the food that had been prepared for him, Kelly went out to fetch two pints of beer. The beer was shared out between the residents, and because there were six other people in the house at the time, more beer was brought in.

As there was a shortage of furniture in the house, most of the people that afternoon were sitting on the floor. Eliza Patten crouched beside Johnson, with her head resting upon his knee and occasionally, they whispered to each other. Although no-one could hear the words that passed between them, they seemed to be on the best of terms. This state of affairs was soon to change.

At about 5 pm, Eliza Patten asked Mrs McCarnon if she could go upstairs to sleep, telling her that she had not slept at all the night before. Mary's husband, Henry McCarnon, a black man, seemingly played no part in the affairs of the brothel. It was said that he worked in Widnes during the week and only came back to Prince William Street at weekends.

Soon after Patten's departure upstairs, Johnson followed her. When Johnson entered the bedroom, he discovered that a young woman by the name of Williams was lying beside Patten. As soon as Johnson came in she left the room, and a few minutes later, Johnson came downstairs and went into the backyard for a while. He then went back upstairs, then yet again returned downstairs, telling Mrs McCarnon that Eliza wanted a smoke.

While Mrs McCarnon was filling a clay pipe for Patten, she came downstairs, bleeding from the nose and with a mark around one eye. When asked how it had happened, Patten, who seemed to be frightened of giving any information, simply said: 'Never mind.' A little while later, she said her injury had been caused by a candlestick. She took the pipe that had been prepared by Mrs McCarnon and began to smoke it. While doing so, she started to cry. It became clear that Johnson had attacked her.

When Johnson, heard these complaints from Patten, he put his hand into a nearby cupboard, brought out a large knife, and stabbed her viciously in the back of her head. The blade penetrated through from her ear to her mouth, cutting the jugular vein. She fell to the floor, whereupon Johnson tried to stab her again.

Henry McCarnon later testified that when this happened he said to Johnson: 'For God's sake, my friend, you had better go out.' It was as if Johnson, instead of killing the woman, had simply created a nasty smell. After wiping the knife blade on his jacket sleeve, Johnson wasted no time in taking to his heels. McCarnon allegedly rushed after him, shouting: 'Police! Police!' As Johnson fled, he threw the knife into a water drain, from which it was recovered the next day. It was left to a neighbour, Mary Carter, who had witnessed Johnson's flight from the scene, to go and fetch two police officers. By this time, Johnson had made his way to the landing stage and had caught a ferry across the Mersey. At about 8 pm that evening, he met an acquaintance called John Donnelly at the top of Queen Street in Birkenhead.

After the two men had shaken hands, Johnson began to cry. In his testimony at the trial on 9th May, Donnelly claimed that Johnson had said to him: 'I have done a murder. On Saturday night I went into a lodging house, and on Sunday morning I went into this house in Prince William Street. I stopped there until the afternoon, and then went upstairs. We had a row. I unscrewed the bottom of a lamp and hit her twice. She said 'Don't murder me go downstairs'. With that I went downstairs. She followed me, and when I seen that, I took the knife and stabbed her.'

Donnelly explained that he went down to the ferry with Johnson, who said: 'Goodbye, the next time I see you will be in the waxworks.'

It seemed at the trial that there was a queue of prosecution witnesses called by Dr Commins, to all of whom Johnson had confessed murder. Johnson, who was unable to give evidence in his own defence, seemed very verbally entangled by the prosecution. None of this evidence was properly challenged by makeshift defence counsel Mr Connell.

John Carter, a carter of Mann Street, said that on the Sunday night at about 8.30 pm he met Johnson in Gore Street and went into a public house with him. Carter, who had already heard of the stabbing, said to Johnson: 'A nice thing you have done for yourself.' Johnson is said to have replied: 'Yes, I am very sorry for it. I liked her as well as my own mother.'

Later that same night, a prostitute called Rebecca Fullerton came across Johnson near park Lane.

'Demon, don't you know me?' She asked him.

'Yes, Jessie', replied Johnson, 'but I didn't like to speak.'

'You have made a nice mess of yourself now', said Becky. When she asked how Eliza Patten was, Johnson told her she was dead.

Fullerton asked him what had happened and the apparently garrulous Johnson issued another confession: 'I can't tell rightly. We had some words upstairs. When I came downstairs I saw the handle of the knife in a cupboard. I took it and struck her. She made her way to the back door, but I could see by the way she held her head that she would die.'

Johnson told Fullerton that he was going to give himself up, but he asked if she would do him a favour. He wanted her to go to 61 Prince William Street and tell them that if anyone asked about it, to either say nothing, or that it was an accident. Johnson offered to shake hands with Rebecca, but she refused to do so.

On Tuesday 25th March, Constable Johnston arrested Johnson in an empty house in Upper Mann Street. He was found in a top garret, lying down on an old mattress, a coat around his shoulders. When taken up by the officer, Johnson apparently said: 'All right, Johnston, she struck me with a candlestick. I will walk with you quietly. I did do it, but I had no intention of doing it.'

In defence of Johnson at his trial, McConnell submitted, probably quite correctly, that the blow which killed Miss Patten was unpremeditated and carried out 'in the heat of passion'. However, such was the amount of deadly force unleashed by Johnson that it was clear that he intended to cause his victim grievous harm, and this implied that he had committed a murder.

McConnell would have known that this was the case and it would have been no surprise to him when the judge, Sir James Stephen, advised the jury to convict Johnson of the capital offence. They took some thirty seconds to do so.

Seconds after hearing the sentence of death, there were histrionics from Thomas Johnson. He threw up his arms, uttered an agonising cry, and fell back into the arms of two warders, who carried him from the dock. The trial had occupied only three hours, being completed by lunchtime.

The execution of Thomas Johnson that occurred on Wednesday 28th May 1879, was the first execution from which press reporters were excluded. Marwood gave Johnson a drop of nine feet two inches, which proved to be satisfactory, allowing the victim a swift oblivion.

A Shocking Death

In 1881, Joseph Patrick McEntee, a tailor, lived with Ellen, his wife of twenty-four years, in a three-storey house at 89 Rose Place, off St Anne Street in Liverpool. At about 10 pm on Monday 4th April, the McEntees were visited by their niece, Catherine Parkinson. Seeing a light, Catherine knocked on the parlour door. From inside the room, her uncle answered: 'I can't find the key'. 'All right, Uncle,' Catherine replied. He then asked her to feel about for the key in the dark lobby. She did so, but could find nothing. McEntee then said, twice over, 'It is better you do not come in'. Catherine, who was used to her uncle's eccentric habits, abandoned her visit and returned home to 53 Pleasant Street.

About half an hour after his niece's visit, McEntee called in at Fanny Birchall's beerhouse at 49 Great Richmond Street. She remembered he was in a hurry and wanted to be served quickly. He took away a pint of ale in a jug. He said that he would pay for it in the morning. Mrs Birchall later recalled that McEntee was rather confused. He seemed, she said, as if he had just woken from a drunken sleep.

There lived on the first floor of the house in Rose Place a couple, William and Martha Pennington, with their little daughter. At 7.30 pm on the Monday evening, the Pennington family went out. They did not return to Number 89 until about 11 pm. On passing the parlour door, which was slightly ajar, Mrs Pennington could see McEntee standing in the room. At about 3 am the Penningtons were awakened by someone knocking on their bedroom door. Martha heard McEntee's voice. When she asked him what he wanted, he said he had stumbled accidentally against the door, and apologised.

Next morning, the Penningtons, wanting to get up at their regular time of 7 am, sent their child downstairs to see what time it was. On coming back, the little girl noticed that the handle of the parlour door was missing. She could not resist peeping through the keyhole. Inside the room, Ellen McEntee was lying on the floor without any clothes on, her hand upon her chest. The girl ran upstairs and told her mother what she had seen. Mrs Pennington went down to see for herself. Sure enough, Mrs McEntee was lying naked, apparently asleep, on the parlour floor.

Martha also noticed that a small piece of bloodstained rag lay in front of the parlour door. Just then, McEntee came downstairs and kicked the rag into the room. Soon afterwards, he left the building.

As soon as McEntee had gone the Penningtons went into the parlour to investigate properly. Mrs McEntee's body had by now been covered by a shawl. They sent for the police. Ellen McEntee's clothes had been torn and scattered about the parlour. Among the clothing was found a piece of paper containing a small amount of money. It was later discovered that Mrs McEntee had pawned her husband's watch.

The Pennington family had lived in the house for only a few weeks. They did not yet realise that Joseph and Ellen were regular heavy drinkers and that Ellen often received violent behaviour from her husband.

At 8 am on that Tuesday morning, Dr John Pickford went to the house and pronounced life extinct. Ellen's body lay on its back, with the legs doubled up under the thighs. The only clothes worn were a pair of stockings. She had sustained head and facial wounds and lay in a pool of blood. A post mortem later revealed several broken ribs. On the left side they had penetrated a lung. Death, said Pickford, was caused by severe shock.

After he left the house, McEntee had travelled to Garston. He went to Joseph Ross' barber's shop and had his beard and moustache shaven off. However, at 10.15 pm that night, McEntee was arrested in Church Road, Garston by Constable William Kee of the Lancashire County Police. He was extremely drunk. The brass knob of the parlour door was found in his pocket. When, next morning, he was charged with killing his wife, McEntee said: 'I know nothing about it.' McEntee was tried for murder on 10th May 1881 before Mr Justice Mathew.

J.B.Aspinall Q.C. led for the Crown. Defence counsel was Dr Commins M.P. Mr Aspinall, as was usual, outlined the facts of the case and called witnesses to prove them. After these witnesses had given their evidence, junior counsel Bremner summed up the case for the prosecution.

In his address to the jury on behalf of McEntee, Dr Commins pointed out that because no-one actually saw Mrs McEntee being attacked, 'the evidence does not show that the prisoner killed her at all, but found her dead. He had acted the way he did from the ordinary instincts of self-preservation.'

Dr Commins also said that 'the whole circumstance of the case rebuts the imputation of malice'. If McEntee had killed his wife 'in a fit of exasperation on finding her in a drunken state, that, of course, cannot be construed as murder.' The case was possibly a little more difficult for the jury because of the lack of an apparent motive. As it was, it only took eighteen minutes to find McEntee guilty as charged. After he was sentenced to death by Mr Justice Mathew, McEntee, who had kept his composure throughout, shook hands with his counsel Dr Commins. He was then taken down to the cells.

Joseph Patrick McEntee was hanged at Kirkdale on Tuesday 31st May 1881. It was now usual to allow for the passage of three Sundays between the sentence of death and its execution. McEntee claimed that he did not know he had killed his wife until he found himself, in the morning, lying beside her dead body.

The press was again excluded. This exclusion had occurred only in Lancashire, where the High Sheriff had rigorously observed the rule. Only the hoisting of the black flag indicated that an execution had taken place. On this occasion, when the flag was raised, the sound of the falling drop could be heard. At that very moment, a nearby railway engine's whistle shrieked shrilly in the morning air.

Marwood allowed a drop of nine feet two inches. Describing the scene outside the prison one reporter wrote that some spectators 'clung with a nervous dread and an almost revolting eagerness to the cold brickwork of the wall, to hear the ghastly thud of the body as it dropped.'

A Harvest Fire

In the summer of 1882, Bernard Mullarkey and three other men had come over from Ireland to gather the harvest at Sumner's Farm in Maghull, north of the city of Liverpool. Incoming farm labourers were usually housed in barns and other outbuildings, often sleeping on the floor or upon beds of rough straw. That summer, Mullarkey, Thomas Cruise, his son Thomas, and a man called Jordan were staying at Sumner's Farm. The latter had come over at harvest time for the last twenty-six years.

At the farm, there was a shippon for the cows and a stable for the horses. Next to these was a large barn with a fire range, above which was a loft, accessible by a ladder. Mullarkey used to sleep by the range while Cruise, young Thomas, and Jordan slept above in the loft.

Mullarkey was on bad terms with the other three men. He and young Thomas used to sleep together down below but Mullarkey had issued threats to the boy, saying he would swing for him. Jordan had also previously slept down below but moved into the loft because of threats from Mullarkey that he would set fire to him and Cruise if they did not leave the farm.

On Friday 23rd September Mullarkey and the other men were at Bradley's beerhouse in Maghull. Within earshot of the men, Mullarkey said to a man called John Cribbin, 'You lot are trying to put the monkey on me, but I will swing for young Cruise and I will put a fire under the building. I will do it. And you will hear of a fire in day or two.'

Just two days later, on Sunday 25th September, Mullarkey and Jordan were in the beerhouse again, with Cribbin. On the way home, Mullarkey asked Jordan to pack up his things and leave the farm. Refusing to be intimidated, Jordan ignored his warnings and said he would not leave. Mullarkey was soon to prove that his repeated warnings were not just idle threats.

Standing at the farm gate on the Sunday night, Mullarkey watched Jordan go indoors. He turned and said to Cribbin: 'I have enough dynamite in my pocket to blow the building up in five minutes. It is red stuff, and I have it in paper.' Cribbin did not believe him.

A few minutes later, Thomas Cruise called out: 'Barney, are you coming to bed?' Mullarkey, however, went into the wash-house while the other three men went to bed in the loft as usual.

During the night, young Thomas was awakened by his father, who was screaming in pain and terror. The boy could see flames raging up the wooden ladder that led to the loft. He woke Jordan, and when they looked out of the window, they saw that the horses were loose in the yard. Mullarkey stood in the middle, fully dressed and shouted at them to jump down.

Eventually, Mullarkey got a ladder to let the men down to safety, but unfortunately it was too late for old Thomas Cruise. Instead of immediately helping the men to escape, Mullarkey had not only released the horses from the stable, but he had also gone to wake the foreman and Mr Sumner. Consequently, the old man had burned to death. Both the loft and the range were gutted and Mullarkey was suspected of having started the fire because of his previous threats. Mr Sumner asked him how the fire had started. He replied: 'As sure as God is in heaven, I don't know. I had nothing at all to do with it.' He was also asked why the horses were let out before any effort was made to rescue the men in the burning loft. Mullarkey simply replied that he was near the horses when the fire started and he had let them out.

On the Monday morning, Mullarkey was arrested and interviewed by Sergeant Heywood. He gave his name as 'Charles Rogers' and explained that he had some drink and then went to sleep in the wash-house. When he awoke he found the place on fire, and he went to fetch Mr Sumner. Trying to take the focus off himself, Mullarkey told the Sergeant that Jordan belonged to a secret society and had committed a murder in Ireland. He said that Jordan had hidden a revolver, but police searches failed to find it.

In custody, on his way from Kirkdale railway station to the gaol, Mullarkey was said to have asked Heywood: 'What will they do to me in this case? Shall I have to swing or get life? I wish I could get off with six months, and then be free from it after. I do not think I shall get to see Maghull again.'

Bernard Mullarkey's murder trial was held on 17th November 1882. The judge was Mr Justice Day. Whilst outlining the case against the accused, Mr Shee was interrupted by a man in the public gallery who called out, in a strong Irish brogue: 'Don't be hard upon him!' The man was quickly removed.

At the end of his opening address, Mr Shee said: 'I must tell the jury that if the prisoner, in attempting to carry out his threats against young Cruise or Jordan, took the life of the old man, he is equally guilty of murder.' When summarising the case for the prosecution, Mrs Shee said it was clear that the fire was not accidental, because none of the men had been smoking. He also pointed out that Mullarkey had previously threatened to burn the men out, and held a grudge against all of them.

Dr Commins, in his speech for the defence, maintained that the prosecution had not made out its case against Mullarkey. He asked the jury to believe that Mullarkey's threats were unconnected to the subsequent fire. The two events, he claimed, were purely coincidental. Commins said: 'The jury knows well that people in the position of the prisoner often use such threatening expressions with no intention of putting them into practice. He had no dynamite, but he had used wild nonsensical language without meaning mischief.' With regard to the actual fire, Dr Commins claimed that it was probable that Cruise, in getting out of bed, might have stepped on a box of matches and started a fire.

Commins accepted that there might be 'strong suspicion of the prisoner's guilt', but this, he said, was not enough. 'The jury must have direct proof that the prisoner committed the crime.' Commins would have known that direct proof was not essential for a conviction. The evidence was circumstantial. He explained: 'In a case of circumstantial evidence, the Crown has to prove that the prisoner had means, motive and opportunity to commit the crime, and secondly that nobody else had.' This was clearly untrue and Commins must have known it.

In his summing up, the mistake was corrected by Mr Justice Day, who said: 'It is idle to talk of circumstantial evidence as though it cannot be relied upon. It is not necessary for the jury to show with certainty that no other person can have done it'. Finally, the judge put this question to the jury: 'As reasonable men, have you been satisfied that the case has been clearly made out against the prisoner?'

The jury returned a guilty verdict after twenty minutes. When asked why the sentence of death should not be passed upon him according to law, Mullarkey replied: 'I am as innocent of that crime as the child unborn, if I never see the face of God in heaven.'

After being sentenced to death, Mullarkey lost his composure. He shouted at the judge: 'You can only judge a fellow on this earth, you can't judge him in the next! You may have to be judged yourself, and may not have as much time to pray for your soul as I have. If I never see the sight of God I am as innocent as the child unborn for what I am going to be hanged for!' He was then taken below.

Mullarkey's execution at Kirkdale on 4th December was strictly private, on the orders of the High Sheriff, Colonel McCorquodale. No reporter was present. The morning was wet and windy. Marwood entered the gaol at 7.15 am. Only about twenty people gathered at the north-west angle of the prison yard. The black flag was raised at 8.03 am and the people dispersed.

Mullarkey's last visitors were two of his cousins from Ireland; his parents, from County Mayo, did not come over to see him. Mullarkey, who said he was nineteen but looked much older, was believed to have been a deserter from the 95th Regiment. The drop was nine feet six inches.

The Runaway

At the Liverpool Winter Assizes of 1883, Henry Dutton, an iron driller aged 23, was charged with the murder of 71-year-old Hannah Hamshaw, who was his wife's grandmother. After Crown counsel Leofric Temple had outlined the facts of the case, he called his first witness. She was Mrs Harriet Kay who lived at 36 St Martin's Cottages in Everton, about five minutes' walk from Mrs Hamshaw's home at 160 Athol Street. At Whitsuntide in 1883, Henry Dutton had married Mrs Hamshaw's 18-year-old granddaughter Charlotte. The couple lived with the grand-mother at Athol Street.

Mrs Kay told the court how, on 6th October, Charlotte Dutton came to her house at about 3 pm. About five minutes later, Henry Dutton arrived at the house.

'What did you run away for?' He asked Charlotte.

'I did not run away from you,' she replied.

'You are a liar.' He snapped back at her.

Mrs Kay and Charlotte went out for about twenty minutes. When they got back at around 4 pm, Dutton had gone.

At about 4.30 pm, after hearing a knock at the door and realising that it was her husband, Charlotte ran into the bedroom, terrified of what he might do to her. Mrs Kay answered the door and Dutton asked her if Charlotte was there. 'Yes, come in, Harry,' she replied.

Dutton was in a raging temper, cursing and swearing. 'I will punish her for what she has done!' He shouted. Mrs Kay went into the bedroom and asked Charlotte to come out. Dutton followed and raised his hand as if to strike his wife. 'No, Harry,' said Mrs Kay, 'you shall not strike her here. This is my house and I will have no striking here!'

After exchanging harsh words, the Duttons left Mrs Kay's house at about 5.45 pm. 'You are a liar', said Dutton to his wife. 'A slap across the mouth is what you want.' On their way home, Mrs Kay went with them as far as Latimer Street, and Dutton was teasing Charlotte, making fun of her appearance and saying she was like an old married woman.

Later on that evening, at about 9 pm, Dutton arrived at Mrs Kay's house again, asking if his wife was there. She told him that she had not seen Charlotte since she left them in Latimer Street. Dutton explained to Mrs Kay that they had quarrelled at the tea table and that Charlotte had left the house.

'The old woman is making mischief between us,' said Dutton.

'No, Harry,' Mrs Kay replied. 'I do not believe that.'

Dutton was in a terrible temper and said: 'I will find Charlotte before eleven o' clock, and so help me God, I will do for one of them before twelve o'clock tonight'.

'Hush, Harry,' she said to him, 'don't say such words as those. I will go with you and see if we can find Charlotte.'

They both left the house and walked to the corner of Athol Street. Here, Dutton asked her to go with him into the public house. Mrs Kay refused and went alone to 160 Athol Street. When she arrived, Old Mrs Hamshaw was standing on the steps at the front door. The two women entered the house but Charlotte was not there. At about 9.30 pm Dutton came home and asked them if they had found his wife. Mrs Kay told him they had not, and he turned and walked out of the house.

At about 10.10 pm Mrs Kay left Mrs Hamshaw alone in the house, promising to come back later. When she returned at about 11 pm she found that Charlotte had arrived. For safety's sake – from the wrath of Dutton – Mrs Kay took Charlotte back to her own house, but Mrs Hamshaw stayed in her home.

Mary Ann Rooney, a widow who lived in the cellar under the Duttons at Athol Street, testified that at about 11.15 pm she heard stamping across the floor above, and heard Mrs Hamshaw cry out: 'Murder!' This then happened again about half an hour later. After the second cry, a crowd had gathered around the front door of the house. Mary Darcy, next door at 158, heard the old woman scream. She knocked on the wall but got no answer. Margaret Greenhalgh, who lived at 162, was asleep when she was disturbed by the rattle of her front window, and then a cry of 'Murder!' This was followed by another, fainter, cry. From her back bedroom, Mrs Greenhalgh was able to look over the dividing yard wall into the scullery of number 60. When she opened the window she could hear Dutton saying to Mrs Hamshaw: 'You know where my wife is, don't you?' The old lady replied that she did not. Dutton told her: 'Don't speak to me like that, or else I will do for you. I shall kick your entrails in.' There was then a faint scream and a dull heavy thud. Margaret went to the front door and shouted to the crowd, seemingly revelling in the tragedy that was unfolding. 'For God's sake,' she cried, 'come to the back. He has murdered her now. She will shout no more!' Margaret ran back to her window. Dutton was in the scullery, shading his eyes from the light and looking to see if the yard was clear. Margaret went back to the front again and called out that Dutton was still in the house. On returning, she saw him locking the scullery door from the outside. In evidence, Mrs Greenhalgh said melodramatically: 'Dutton ran out through the back door like a flash of lightning'.

In his testimony, James Kay, Harriet's husband, described how at about 11.40 pm he had gone to Dutton's front door and found a great crowd of people around it. He knocked several times without getting an answer but then he heard someone walking in the lobby.

'Harry!' He called out to Dutton.

'Is that you, Jim?' He replied.

'Open the door,' Kay said. 'Not to let that crowd in. No-one will come in but me.' Kay knocked again. Receiving no answer, he tried to break open the door, but could not manage it. He then went round the back of the house and found the yard door open, but the scullery door locked. He broke the kitchen window, unlatched it, and climbed into the house. In the doorway between the kitchen and the scullery sat Mrs Hamshaw. Kay lifted her head. He could then see that the lower part of her face, from the nose downwards, was covered in blood.

A female neighbour had followed Kay through the window and she helped him to lay the old lady on a sofa. 'She is alive', said the neighbour. Kay then went for Dr Sheldon and a few minutes after he arrived, Hannah Hamshaw died.

Dutton was hiding out at the house of Mr and Mrs Whitehead at 13 Tyndal Street. Initially, he went there at around 10.45 pm and stayed for about half an hour. He returned not long after midnight and ate supper. When the Whiteheads' son Joseph came in Dutton asked him if there was a crowd around his front door. 'Not much', replied Joseph, 'but it is gathering'. Asked what he had done to the old lady, Dutton said: 'I gave her a shove and she fell.'

Dr Sheldon, at the trial, testified that Mrs Hamshaw was a mass of cuts and bruises. He attributed death to the rupture of blood vessels in the brain, external violence, and the resultant shock to the system.

Police Constable Samuel Gracey, who was on duty in Athol Street, went to the Whiteheads' house at 1.20 am. Dutton was found hiding in a cupboard under the stairs and when he was arrested, he said: 'I know nothing about it. I only shoved her, and left her sitting in the chair.'

At the trial, defence counsel Shand wanted the jury to return a verdict of manslaughter, saying that there was no intention to commit murder. 'The prisoner may,' said Shand, 'in a fit of almost mental aberration, have struck the woman an unguarded blow, causing her to fall in some sharp corner.'

After half an hour, the jury found Dutton guilty of murder. Before the sentence of death was passed, Dutton said: 'I asked her where my wife was. She said she did not know. I pushed her, and she fell backwards, and she fell on her left side. I picked her up and put her in a chair. She told me to go out for my wife, and I went out to find her, but could not find her. On my way home I called at Mr Whitehead's, and stayed there.'

On 3rd December 1883, Henry Dutton was executed by Bartholomew Binns at Kirkdale. It was a cold, raw morning, drizzling with rain, and the procedure went very badly wrong. Binns used a rope that was twice the thickness of the one Marwood generally used. The drop was seven feet five inches, and when Dutton fell, the rope slipped round to the back of his neck, which was not dislocated by the fall. Dutton moved his pinioned arms convulsively, repeatedly opening and closing his hands. His legs moved rapidly and violently, showing the terrible agony he was suffering. He uttered no sound during the hopeless struggle that lasted for about two minutes. After eight minutes his pulse had stopped.

Black Widows

In 1880, two sisters – 50-year-old Catherine Flannagan and 40-year-old Margaret Thompson – lived at 5 Skirving Street. Both women were widows, and they resided with Catherine's son, John Flannagan, aged 22, and her daughter, Ellen Flannagan, who was aged ten. Also in the cramped dwelling lived a widower called Thomas Higgins, along with his daughter Mary, aged eight. The household total was made up to nine by a dock labourer called Patrick Jennings, his 12-year-old son Patrick Junior and his daughter Margaret Jennings, who was 16.

Over a period of several years, four of the nine residents died, as the result of a series of evil and callous murders by the secret administration of poison.

The first fatality occurred on 7th December 1880, when Catherine's son John Flannagan passed away. The next to die was little Mary Higgins who passed away on 29th November 1882. Margaret Thompson had recently become the young girl's stepmother after she married Mary's father, becoming Mrs Higgins. Margaret Jennings, nursed by Mrs Flannagan and Mrs Higgins, died on 25th January 1883. After suffering with diarrhoea for three weeks, Thomas Higgins died on October 2nd 1883. It was this death – the last in a dreadful series – which was to result in the exposure of a ruthless poisoning plot.

Early in 1883, the sisters had moved from Skirving Street to a house at 105 Latimer Street. On September 22nd of that year, Margaret and Thomas Higgins moved into the cellar of 27 Ascot Street, a few minutes walk from Catherine Flannagan's house.

After Thomas Higgins' death, his brother Patrick became suspicious, not least because Thomas had always seemed to be a strong and healthy man. Never before had Thomas suffered from the stomach and bowel trouble that had killed him. The doctor's certificate gave the cause of death as dysentery.

Patrick discovered that his brother had been insured for over £100, and on the advice of local doctor Whitford, he visited the coroner. A coach set out for 27 Ascot Street. Inside were Patrick, Dr Whitford, and Dr Limerick, together with Mr Hargreaves, an official beadle from the office. When they arrived, funeral coaches were standing outside number 27. Dr Whitford had authority from the coroner to stop the funeral taking place and also to carry out a thorough examination of the body. A gang of drunken women was thrown out of the house and the undertaker's coach horses were returned to their stables with empty loads. Wasting no time, Dr Whitford, helped by Dr Limerick, laid out Higgins' body on the cellar table and carried out a post mortem.

They found that the internal organs were profoundly inflamed, which indicated the effect of an irritant poison. The same day, at the Royal Institution in Colquitt Street, Edward Davies analysed the body samples. He concluded that Higgins had been killed by the administration of poison, namely arsenic in solution.

Catherine Flannagan and Margaret Higgins were both arrested – Margaret on 9th October and Catherine on 15th October. When charged with the murder of her husband, Mrs Higgins said: 'I know nothing at all about it. I went for his medicine at Burlington Street dispensary and I gave it to him as I got it.'

When Mrs Flannagan was charged, she replied tersely: 'I never knew nothing about it. I never did it and I know nobody else that did.'

Before the trial, Catherine Flannagan laid the blame for the poisonings on her sister. She even offered to turn Queen's evidence and testify against Margaret in return for her own freedom.

The trial opened on St Valentine's Day, 1884 at St George's Hall. The sisters were indicted on three counts – for the murders of Margaret's husband Thomas Higgins, of Margaret Jennings and of Catherine's son John. Higgins was also charged separately with the murder of her young stepdaughter Mary. Leading for the Crown was the Recorder of Liverpool, Mr J.B. Aspinall. The defence of both prisoners was in the hands of Mr Shee and Mr Pickford and the judge was Mr Justice Butt.

Mr Aspinall said that the Crown would be seeking a conviction only on the single charge relating to Thomas Higgins. He pointed out that during the last year of his life, Thomas had been insured, chiefly without his knowledge, with no fewer than five different companies. Thus it was the death benefits that provided the motive for his murder. The prisoners had been the only people to attend to Higgins throughout his fatal illness. Furthermore, arsenic was found in a medicine bottle recovered from Ascot Street and fluff and dust containing traces of arsenic was present in samples taken from Mrs Higgins' smock pocket. The Crown alleged that the arsenic found in body was taken from fly-papers containing the poison. Each paper contained the best part of a grain of arsenic.

When he closed the case for the prosecution, Mr Aspinall, anticipating that defence counsel Shee would later be criticizing the uncertainty of the forensic evidence, stressed to the jury that even before the recent introduction of new methods of chemical analysis, the amount of arsenic found in Higgins' body was sufficiently large enough to have caused his death.

Defence counsel Shee's task, in convincing the jury that the case had not been proven beyond reasonable doubt, was a laborious one. He began his speech by pointing out that Mrs Flannagan's six-day flight from justice should not be taken as evidence of her guilt. He launched into his argument:

> The learned friend for the prosecution seems almost to imagine that he is not in court of justice, but within the precincts of a gaol, with the rag raised to show that these two poor women had been sacrificed to public prejudice. Run away? Why should Mrs Flannagan not run away? Mrs Mackenzie had read to her from a newspaper about 'The Wholesale Poisoning Case' and somebody had said that it would be a case for hangman Marwood's successor. Was that not enough to frighten the strongest and bravest man who ever lived, much less an old woman fifty to sixty years of age?

It appeared that Mr Shee hoped that the jury, not being versed in science, might reject the medical evidence as simply speculation, which they could not properly assess for themselves. Mr Shee said:

> Scientific evidence, I care not who gives it, might assist a jury, and it is right that it should, but the jury themselves must find the verdict. We will never be content in this country to have men tried by juries of lawyers, Royal Academicians, or experts in handwriting, for our lives and liberties will never be safe if we are to depend upon the enthusiasm and theories of skilled witnesses.

He continued:

What do their tests come to and how much arsenic did they say they found in the bodies? In one case about three grains, in the second about two grains, and in the next, six one-hundredths. None says that is a poisonous dose. I ask the jury whether they are satisfied that there was any arsenic at all in Thomas Higgins' body? Might not this amount have come from the laboratories?

The conclusion of Mr Shee's address to the jury seemed to end on a rather flat note. He said:

In conclusion, I make a strong appeal to you, to remember that your verdict, unlike a civil verdict, is not subject to any appeal. If the prisoners are found guilty, I believe there will not be a single voice to raise them from the penalty which must follow, whereas, if I am right in my theory for the defence, there is another chance of trying the prisoners for the deaths of other persons.

In his remarks to the jury, Mr Justice Butt criticised the practice of issuing life insurance policies where the person being insured was unaware and unable to consent. The judge said:

Unless their proceedings are placed upon a sounder system, considerable danger must result. It makes one ask the question: how many people might there be lying in the burial rounds of this and other large towns who, if their lives had never been insured, might have been living at this moment?

It took the jury fifty minutes to decide that both women were guilty of the murder of Thomas Higgins. After being sentenced to death, Mrs Higgins fainted. Mrs Flannagan showed no emotion at all. During the trial, Higgins had wept at intervals in the dock, frequently dabbing her eyes with a handkerchief. Flannagan, according to a *Liverpool Mercury* reporter, 'maintained an air of stolid indifference, apparently unconcerned and taking no intelligent interest in the proceedings.'

The double hanging of the Flannagan and Higgins sisters took place on 3rd March 1884. At 7.58 am, a procession of officials, together with the two condemned women and the hangman, emerged from a doorway into the open air of Kirkdale Prison yard. Snow and sleet were falling and the wind blew in cold, fitful blasts. Bareheaded and dazed, the two women were helped up the twenty-two steps onto the scaffold.

Flannagan stood silent and ghastly pale, contrasted with Higgins, whose face was flushed red as her eyes darted around her. The bolts were drawn and, with a sickening thud, the sisters dropped together into instant oblivion, their spinal cords immediately severed. Higgins' head jerked sharply three or four times.

The two doctors in attendance announced to reporters that the heartbeats had ceased precisely seven minutes after the drop, although the women were already unconscious. Executioner Binns revealed that Mrs Flannagan, who was four feet eleven inches tall and considerably heavier than her sister, was allowed a drop of ten feet nine inches. Mrs Higgins, who was four inches taller, dropped eleven feet and three quarters of an inch. Mrs Flannagan was survived by her daughter Ellen and at the sisters' request, the girl had been the only visitor whom either had received while they awaited their awful fate.

'Knives, Boys!'

A few days after the Flannagan and Higgings sisters had been sentenced to death, Mr Justice Butt was on the bench again, hearing the trial of five young men for the murder of a Spanish seaman in Regent Road, alongside the Liverpool North Docks. The five men accused at St George's Hall on the morning of Monday 18th February 1884 were: Michael McLean, 18, a labourer; Patrick Duggan, 18, a scaler; Alexander Campbell, 20, a barber; William Dempsey, 19, a labourer, and Murdoch Ballantyne, 20, a labourer. They were jointly charged with having murdered Exequiel Rodriguez Nuniez on Saturday 5th January 1884.

At about 10 pm on that day, Nuniez and another Spanish sailor were returning along Regent Road to their ship in Canada Dock. At the junction with Blackstone Street they encountered the five prisoners. One of the prisoners attacked Nuniez, whilst Ballantyne struck the other sailor in the face, cutting his lip. The two sailors fled in opposite directions but unfortunately for Nuniez, he was overtaken by the prisoners in Regent Road. Here, he was kicked, beaten with belts and very badly injured. He managed, however, to escape and ran into a passage in Fulton Street.

When Nuniez returned to Regent Road, the chase was again taken up by the prisoners. Crying out, 'Knives, boys, knives!' they caught up with Nuniez again, opposite the Fulton Street Foundry. Again, Nuniez was kicked, knocked down and badly beaten.

After a second escape from the clutches of his attackers, Nuniez was eventually caught under the railway arch at the corner of Blackstone Street. It was here that McLean and Duggan were seen to use knives on Nuniez before abandoning him as he lay dying.

Police Constable Evans arrived on the scene and seeing that Nuniez was seriously hurt, had him taken to the Northern Hospital. He was found to be dead on arrival. Nuniez had sustained a wound on the lower part of his neck, together with two less serious cuts on his back. The neck wound was judged to be in itself sufficient to have caused death, but Nuniez actually died from loss of blood in the region of the heart.

When the body was initially searched by Evans, a sheath knife was found hidden under the dead man's jersey, between the shoulder blades. It did not appear that Nuniez had drawn the knife in an effort to defend himself. Crown counsel Mr Potter Q.C. said there seemed to be no clear motive for the attack. He said: 'The whole assault was a piece of wanton brutality.'

After the killing, Dempsey and Campbell went with Ballantyne to Dempsey's home. Dempsey asked his mother for a brush to clean blood off his trousers, explaining that he and Campbell had been sparring, and that he had made Campbell's nose bleed. The following day, Mrs Dempsey pawned the trousers. When they were later redeemed by the police, they were found to be damp and still bloodstained.

When McLean was arrested on the morning of 6th January, he appeared to drop a knife. Two other knives were found on him, and all the weapons were said to have been bloodstained.

It soon became clear from lack of evidence that some members of the gang of five were more culpable than others. Mr Potter told the jury: 'It is for you to decide whether the prisoners, or which of them, have the crime with which they were charged brought home to them.'

Summing up, Mr Justice Butt said he could not believe that the fatal stab in the back of the neck was done in self-defence. He said that the evidence against Campbell, Dempsey and Ballantyne was 'feeble' and advised acquittals for them. After fifty minutes, the jury returned a verdict of 'wilful murder against McLean and Dugan'. Dempsey, Campbell and Ballantyne were found not guilty and were released.

Before being sentenced to death, McLean and Dugan both blamed Dempsey for the murder. With callous smiles on their faces, the two condemned men walked jauntily from the dock. Dugan's sentence was later commuted by the Home Secretary to one of life imprisonment.

The execution of McLean's sentence on 10th March was marred by the dreadful conduct of hangman Bartholomew Binns. He was drunk when he reached Kirkdale and police had to be called to restrain him. The prison governor took the precaution of contacting Samuel Heath, who waited on stand-by. Despite Heath's presence, Binns made a mess of the execution, only giving McLean a drop of nine feet six inches. Fortunately, however, the drop broke his neck instantaneously. Binns was dismissed from the list of executioners appointed by the Home

Office. The foreman of the inquest jury said 'Binns does not seem to be a fit and proper person to carry out these executions. He was in a beastly state of drunkenness when he presented himself, and he deserves censure for that also.'

It was said that the chaplain, Father Bonte, believed in McLean's innocence throughout the trial. On the gallows, McLean said: 'Gentlemen, I consider it a disgrace to the police force of Liverpool and the laws of the country that I am going to suffer death, and another boy is going to suffer imprisonment for life, for a crime of which we are both innocent, as God is my judge.'

Bludgeoned to Death

At the Summer Assizes of 1884, tinsmith Peter Cassidy, aged 54, was charged with the murder of his wife Mary. Prosecuting counsel was Hon. A. D. Eliot and defence counsel was Mr McConnell. The judge was Mr Justice Day.

The offence was alleged to have taken place in a rooming house at 9 Howe Street, off Derby Road in Bootle. Prosecutor Eliot called upon three witnesses, all of whom lived in the house, to prove that not only did Cassidy kill his wife, but also that be had previously threatened that he would do so. According to Eliot, Mary Cassidy's death was not a incidental act of violence but was premeditated by Cassidy because Mary, instead of paying her way, had run into debt.

The first prosecution witness was Mrs Jane Edwards. She testified that the Cassidys moved into the house in December 1883. They occupied the front part of the top landing, while Mrs Edwards lived in the back part.

After being away from the house for several days because of a disagreement with her husband, Mary Cassidy returned on Wednesday 25th June. Mrs Edwards testified that Mary went into the back parlour, and was 'all of a tremble' with drink. She asked for a glass of beer, but Mrs Edwards refused. 'No,' she told Mary, 'I will give you a cup of tea.' This did not satisfy Mary, who replied, 'No, I can't drink that. Give me three halfpence for a glass of beer, and if God spares me I will never take beer again.' Jane did then bring Mary some beer. Mary drank it and then left Jane's room.

Patrick McGee, a ship's fireman, also gave evidence at the trial. He lived in the front part of the first floor, and the Cassidys lived above him, on the top floor.

Peter Cassidy was employed by the Cunard Company, and often worked at night. Just before midnight on 25th June, McGee heard

Cassidy say to his wife, 'You are a fine woman. I have been at Manchester looking for you'. He asked his wife to get his dinner ready and clean the place out. 'I am not able', replied Mary. She had asked Mrs McGee to bring her a pint of beer, but she told Mary: 'Don't take it. A cup of tea will do you more good.' Mary replied, 'never mind, child,' and drank the beer anyway. Then the husband and wife shook hands and Peter Cassidy said: 'What is done, let it be done, and no more about it.' It appeared as if the couple had settled their differences.

However, only five minutes later, Mr McGee heard something fall to the floor with a bang. He went upstairs and saw that part of the Cassidy's door was broken. Mary was on the floor beside the bed, and was bleeding from a head wound. Cassidy, standing next to his wife, confessed to McGee: 'I have done it, Mr McGee. I am willing to stand by it.' McGee went to fetch a police officer.

Jane Edwards had heard the shouting from her own room and was so frightened that she ran out of the house. Having calmed down a little, she returned into the house and shouted up the stairs to Cassidy, 'What have you done?'

'Do not come up here. I have done it and I cannot help it' Cassidy replied.

'What have you done?' asked Jane again.

He shouted to her: 'I have done it. Do not come up. I am waiting for an officer.'

Jane told him that she wanted to go up to get some clean pinafores for her children. Cassidy told her, 'You cannot come up, nor anybody else, unless they bring on officer.' He was holding a piece of lead piping in his hand.

In order to prove that Cassidy's attack on his wife was premeditated, prosecuting counsel Eliot called upon Hyman Swift to give evidence. Swift was a furniture dealer who lived in the house. He had taken some furniture back from the Cassidys because they could not pay the instalments as they fell due. When Cassidy heard about his wife's failure to pay, he had said to Swift, 'The first time I get hold of her, I will do for her.'

After the attack on Mary, Cassidy told Swift that if he came upstairs he would kill him. 'I have done it', he said, 'and I will go to the scaffold like a good lad.' Tactlessly, Swift asked him: 'Won't you be sorry?' Cassidy replied: 'I am never sorry for what I do. If you don't go down, I don't think so much of your life as a cockroach.'

Cassidy told the police that he had killed Mary with a mallet. Her skull had been fractured and three out of the six scalp wounds went right through her skull. A bloodstained mallet lay in an open box near Cassidy's door and hidden in the room, behind some boards, a bloodstained cleaver was found. When Cassidy was charged with murder at Bootle police station by Constable Jamieson, he said: 'Well, I do not know what to say about it. I am sorry it happened.'

With regard to Cassidy's threats to kill his wife, defence barrister McConnell said that 'they cannot be construed as establishing premeditation for such threats are unfortunately too often used by that class of persons.' He read out a statement made by Cassidy. It said:

> I asked her to clean the place up and I would make a fire. She said: "I am damned if I will clean a place like this." I got the cleaver to cut some firewood and I said: "You only come here to get McGee's money and then you go away again." While my head was turned to cut wood, she struck me on the back of the head with the mallet, causing it to bleed. I have the mark on my head now. I turned and struck her on the head with the cleaver. I had no intention of causing her death.

If Cassidy were telling the whole truth, he might have got away with manslaughter owing to provocation. However, Mary Cassidy had been injured six times. McConnell could do little else than ask the jury for a manslaughter verdict. The trial was over before lunch. The jury retired at 12.30 pm and returned to court at 1.05 pm, strongly recommending Cassidy to mercy. Cassidy had nothing to say. He was sentenced to death.

Peter Cassidy was hanged at Kirkdale on 19th August 1884. While he was being pinioned, the prison clock stopped. As a result, the reporters only just avoided missing the execution altogether.

Berry of Bradford performed well. The rope used was made of Italian hemp and was a thickness of 5/8th inch, favoured by Marwood. Cassidy went into immediate oblivion with a drop of eight feet nine inches. His heart stopped beating after five minutes.

Sailor's Revenge

Early in January 1884, John Hamblin set sail for Australia. During the sailor's previous voyages, his wife Elizabeth, left free to pursue her immoral ways, lived with other seamen in the house, at 3 Anson Place, off Liverpool's London Road.

In September 1884, Ernest Ewerstadt, a Russian seaman, had been living with Lizzie Hamblin for several months. Unfortunately for him, he had run short of money, which resulted in Lizzie barring him from the house. Ernest was hurt and angry at being rejected by her and his anger was intensified by the fact that other sailors – some of them black – had been seen at the house. Ernest's inability to dissipate his angry feelings was to have a tragic sequel at Anson Place.

After living with Lizzie, Ernest went to lodge with John Prange at Prange's father's house. On the evening of Friday 19th September, the two men went out together. When they were at Lime Street station, Ernest asked Prange to go with him to Anson Place to see Lizzie. On their way they saw two Negroes in Church Street that Ernest recognised from Lizzie's house. When he asked them to see her, the men threatened to stab him, and said if he wanted to see Lizzie, he would have to come to the house.

When they arrived, Ernest suggested that Prange go in and ask Lizzie to come out and speak to him, and to assure her that he would not harm her. In the house, Prange found Lizzie with the two men. She refused to come out and speak to Ernest and when Prange told him the bad news, Ernest said, 'Never mind, I will buy a revolver.'

According to Ellen Slater, who lived opposite Lizzie Hamblin, Ernest had also tried to talk to Lizzie a fortnight earlier. She saw Ernest knock on the door of Number 3 and when Lizzie saw who it was she had tried to shut the door again, but Ernest had managed to force his way in.

On Saturday 20th September, the day after Prange's visit, Mrs Slater saw Lizzie and Ernest in a public house on Gildart Street at around 8 pm. Lizzie said to Mrs Slater: 'Here's Ernest'. He pulled out a dagger and showed the woman.

'Mrs Slater, what do you think of that?' He said.

'Don't show me anything like that,' she snapped back at him.

Ernest said: 'I am going to do a bloody deed in this street tonight.' On hearing this, Lizzie stepped back a little and gave a slight laugh, but did not seem overly alarmed by what Ernest had said. In retrospect, she should have taken his remarks much more seriously.

Mrs Slater went home, followed by Lizzie and Ernest. On the way, Lizzie asked Mrs Slater for a few matches, saying she was going to get some tobacco for Ernest. While she was gone, Mrs Slater was alone in her house with Ernest, and once again, he pulled out the knife. When she told him to put it away, he repeated his threat to 'do a deed' in the street that night. He kept playing with the dagger, pulling it in and out of his pocket, until eventually, he was persuaded by Mr and Mrs Slater to leave the house.

Later on, Mrs Slater went shopping. When she came back, she was told by a neighbour that there was something wrong at Number 3. She went to Lizzie's house and when she entered she found her lying on the floor. Her feet were pointing to the fireplace and her head towards the outer wall.

Mrs Slater said to her, 'How is this, Lizzie?' The woman raised her hands, moaned pitifully, and rolled over towards the window. Mrs Slater knelt beside her and asked her what was wrong. It was then that she noticed that Lizzie's chest was covered in blood. The stab wound had penetrated her heart.

Ernest Ewerstadt was tried at the assizes before Mr Justice Day and a jury in November 1884. Ewerstadt, an English speaker, pleaded not guilty. He had told Prange that he would buy a revolver, but instead he had bought a dagger. A musician called William Gillicky had gone with Ernest to buy the dagger from a shop in Park Lane. Shopkeeper Michael Kelly testified that the dagger produced in court by Crown counsel Mr Temple Q.C. was the one he had sold to Ernest. It bore the inscription: *Never draw me without reason or sheath me without honour.*

Mr Temple called upon several local children to give evidence of what they saw and heard at 3 Anson Place on Saturday 20th September. Henry Vickock, a 12-year-old boy who lived at Upper Anson Terrace, said that he saw Ernest and Lizzie go into her house. Then peeping through the door, which was slightly ajar, the boy saw Ernest grasp Lizzie by the throat, holding a knife in his other hand. He was asking her for three halfpence, saying that if she did not give it to him he would kill her.

Henry Titherington, aged 10, had seen Ernest climbing over Lizzie's back wall. When he looked under the front door, he heard Ernest ask Lizzie if she would have a drink. At first she said no, but then changed her mind. Then they went into the parlour, where the boy saw Ernest strike Lizzie a blow on the left breast. She fell backwards. The other boys that were on the step with Henry burst the door open, and called for help from a neighbour, Mrs Rylands, who was walking down Anson Place.

The third child witness was 14-year-old Ann Davies. She said that she had looked under the door and saw Lizzie lying on the floor. A man whom she later identified as Ernest was standing by Lizzie with a knife in his hand.

Ernest had not made a very positive attempt to escape from the scene. Mary-Jane Taylor testified that she was standing at the corner of Anson Place and London Road when Ernest approached her and said: 'Me kill my Lizzie. I will die too.'

Police Constable Robinson met Ernest as he was walking from Anson Place into London Road and immediately arrested him. When charged with murder, Ernest said, 'I know nothing about it.' The fatal dagger was found under the seat of a lavatory in the yard. The weapon was in a sheath and when he drew it, Constable Allison found blood on four inches of the blade.

Ernest claimed that he had been drunk and had fought with the two Negroes, but did not know how Lizzie came to be slain. Junior prosecuting counsel McConnell read out a statement that Ernest had made in the magistrates' court, before he was committed for assizes trial. The statement said: 'I remember I was drunk. I was fighting with two dark chaps, and if you find out that I have done it I will die for it. The dark chaps had daggers as well. It was just like a dream to me the morning I woke in prison.'

At the end of the prosecution case, Mr Temple briefly addressed the jury. Then defence counsel Mr Segar said that there had been a quarrel between Ernest and the black men. He claimed that Lizzie had met her death 'more by misadventure than design'. Mr Segar described the children's evidence as unreliable. He denied that the boy Titherington could have seen the blow struck by looking under the front door. He submitted the possibility that during a fight with the black men, Mrs Hamblin met her death while shielding Ernest from a dagger blow.

In his summing up, Mr Justice Day told the jury that there was no evidence of the black men being seen in the neighbourhood of Anson Place, nor of the 'struggle or scuffle' which defence counsel had suggested. The judge said: 'There is not a tittle of evidence of this theory, nor of the presence of anyone else save the man and the woman.'

After twelve minutes, the jury brought in a guilty verdict. Sentence of death was pronounced. Ewerstadt, having said that he wished to speak, uttered only a few words in broken English. Unfortunately, he was inaudible to those watching the proceedings.

Ernest Ewerstadt was hanged on Monday 8th December 1884. Attended by the Reverend Krusmann, pastor of the Lutheran Church in Renshaw Street, Ewerstadt protested his innocence to the last breath.

Although the weather that morning was fine, only about a hundred onlookers gathered outside Kirkdale Prison. A reporter wrote, 'The black flag has been hoisted so frequently of late at Kirkdale Jail that even the ill-conditioned loiterers are apparently getting tired of the miserable spectacle.'

The hanging – supervised by Berry of Bradford and assisted by a young man called Speight – went badly wrong. Ewerstadt was allowed a drop of seven feet and eight inches. Because the rope was too short, he died from slow strangulation rather than from the dislocation of the neck. In spite of this glaring deficiency, the inquest jury decided that 'the law had been carried out in a proper manner.'

An Unfortunate Shot

On 9th September 1885, in a public house on Beaufort Street, Toxteth Park, George Thomas, a coloured seaman, shot dead a woman called Margaret Askin. A few months later, having confessed to the crime, Thomas was hanged at Kirkdale on Tuesday 8th December 1885.

Maggie Askin, who had been widowed for eleven years, lived in 2 Court, Brassey Street, with a woman called Mrs Tipping. Askin, a prostitute, belonged to a class of women known to the Victorians as 'unfortunates', earning their living from men, particularly sailors who had been paid off in Liverpool after a voyage.

Such a man was George Thomas. He used to stay with Maggie until his money ran short. On Thursday 3rd September, Thomas disembarked at Liverpool from Bombay. He was paid the next day and stayed with Maggie for two days. On Monday the 7th, she told him he could not stay with her any longer, because she was expecting the arrival of another sailor, Louis Powell. On Tuesday the 8th, Thomas visited a pawnbroker where he exchanged his watch for a revolver, using the name Lewis. He told the pawnbroker that he wanted to take the firearm to sea on his next voyage.

On the same day, Thomas visited Maggie, quarrelled with her, and struck her on the shoulder. Powell separated them, and Thomas struck him as well so Powell challenged Thomas to a fight. They went into the street and fought a couple of rounds, after which Powell went back to his boarding house.

At about 2.15 pm on Wednesday 9th September, Thomas called at Brassey Street. Powell, Maggie and Mrs Tipping were there and Thomas complained to Powell that Maggie had three pounds belonging to him. When Thomas continued to grumble about the debt, Powell paid him out of his own pocket.

At abut 8.30 pm that evening, now having funds, Thomas asked his companions to go out for a drink. Powell refused, but the two women went with him to a pub in Beaufort Street. After a while, he sent Mrs Tipping to fetch Powell, but he still refused to come.

When Mrs Tipping got back to the pub, she found Thomas and Maggie in the bar parlour. Maggie was seated and Thomas was standing and she noticed that Thomas had a glass of port whilst Maggie had ginger beer.

Out of the blue, Thomas drew a revolver, reached across the table and fired it at Maggie. She called out: 'Oh, Polly, I am shot!' and then 'Powell, where are you?' When she called out Powell's name, Thomas snarled at her: 'I will make you no good for Powell or anybody else!' He fired again, this time striking Maggie in the forehead. A third shot hit her in the mouth. When his victim fell dead, Thomas turned the gun on himself and fired into his temple. Miraculously, he survived. A bullet was later found beneath the skin of the temple, but the injury was not serious.

When a policeman entered, summoned by the pub manager, Thomas said to him: 'I did it, officer. I will go with you.' At the Southern Hospital, where he was examined, Thomas said, 'I am sorry I did not polish myself off with her.'

On 16th November George Thomas came for trial at St George's Hall before Mr Justice Wills and a jury. By now, Thomas had confessed to the crime but nevertheless he pleaded not guilty, thereby laying the responsibility on the prosecution to prove murder. In his defence, Dr Commins claimed that there was absence of motive. He asked the jury to conclude that Thomas had suffered a fit of temporary insanity.

Mr Justice Wills summed up and Thomas was found guilty after ten minutes' consultation by the jury. Before being sentenced to death, Thomas was allowed to read out a statement. He said:

> All I have to say is that I that I am very sorry I have not shot the whole family, for I have been kicked about by them for some time. Both man and woman ill-treated me and I could not hold my passion. I left the woman's place and she sent after me with a young girl. Then she came after me and knocked a bottle of pickles out of my hand and broke it. I could not hold my passion. This was on the Monday night. On Tuesday morning she said to me: 'Thomas, give me a pound to buy some fruit for my boy'. I went to the bank and got some money and gave it to her. She said to me: "If you see Louis Powell in my house do

not say anything to him." I had some words with her, and she jumped at me. I said "Maggie, what are you doing?" She picked up a cup and struck me with it. Powell also turned on me and kicked me into the street. I could not do otherwise than buy the revolver. I said to the pawnbroker: "How much for the revolver?" He said 'Eleven shillings." I said I had not got enough, and was leaving the shop when he said: "Young man, you had better leave something on this, it is a splendid revolver." I said: "Here is my watch. Keep it. I shall get some money out of the bank tomorrow and then I will get my watch." On Wednesday I went and saw Margaret and she asked me for six pounds. I said I would give her three, but she was not content with that, and she jumped up and took her part. At night I went there again, and I was again treated ill. As I was going away, I turned to Margaret and said I would see her tomorrow. She said: "Thomas, if you do not see me tonight, you shall not see me any more." I asked her and Mrs Toping to come and have a drink, and they came. I have letters to show that Margaret wanted me to marry her, but I did not want to marry. Before I went on my last voyage, I left my watch and some shirts with her, and when I came back I found she had pawned them. She gave me back the ticket for the watch, but she kept the shirts to encumber me to the place. I am only sorry I did not shoot Powell and the others.

After being sentenced to death, Thomas said cheerfully: 'Praise God for that. I shall have no more suffering on earth.' He then walked jauntily down the steps leading to the cells.

The execution of George Thomas took place on 8th December 1885 at Kirkdale. Thomas, who was born in Demerara, was five feet ten inches tall with a powerful athletic build. Hangman Berry allowed a drop of seven feet eleven inches. As Berry stooped to pinion his legs, Thomas said: 'Take warning by me, all you young men. Beware of the sins of adultery and murder. I have committed a grievous sin in the sight of God.'

Dr Barr, the prison surgeon, said that although Thomas' heart beat for fifteen minutes after the drawing of the bolt, total unconsciousness was instantaneous, because the vertebrae of the neck had been dislocated. As was usual, the body was allowed to hang for an hour before being cut down.

Poisonous Mother

As the new year of 1887 approached, a 31-year-old widow called Elizabeth Berry was working as a nurse in the Oldham workhouse. Mrs Berry had had two children. One of them died in 1884. The surviving daughter, Edith Annie Betty, aged 11, had not lived with Mrs Berry for some years, but with a couple called Saunderson at Miles Platting.

On Monday December 27th 1886, Mrs Berry went to Mrs Saunderson's house and stayed there until December 29th. She then left for the Oldham workhouses taking with her Edith and a girl called Beatrice Hall, to spend their holiday there.

Next to Mrs Berry's sitting room in the workhouse was a surgery. It was here that drugs were stored. Although many poisonous compounds like arsenic solution were kept under lock and key, there were many other poisonous substances on open shelves.

On New Year's Day 1887, at about 9.30 a.m., a woman called Dillon saw young Edith going from her mother's bedroom to the sitting room. Then, at about 10.15 a.m., Dillon saw Mrs Berry and Edith on their own in the surgery. On going into the sitting room at about 10.45 a.m., she found Edith leaning against her mother, vomiting. Dillon noticed that Mrs Berry had a tumbler of liquid in her hand and Edith was pleading, 'Oh, Mamma, I cannot drink it'.

Later on that day, a woman called Ellen Thompson saw Edith vomiting continually for about five minutes. Dr Patterson, the workhouse surgeon, was called in. He prescribed a mixture of iron and quinine and had Edith removed to sleep in her mother's bedroom. Mrs Berry stayed with her daughter all night and refused anyone who offered to help with the child.

On the Sunday morning, Dr Patterson found that the girl looked better. He noticed that one of the towels which Edith had used had a distinctly acidic smell. At about 2.00 p.m. that day, when Edith was asleep, Ellen Thompson noticed a blister on the child's upper lip. When Mrs Berry was asked about it, she said that she had been giving Edith an orange and sugar and she supposed that the orange might have caused the blister.

For part of the Sunday afternoon, Mrs Berry was left alone with her daughter. At about 5.20 p.m., a workhouse official came to stay in the room. Edith was vomiting frequently and the blister on her lips had developed into a series of larger dark marks; suspicion arose that the mother had been feeding some sort of acidic poison to her child.

Later that evening, Edith was visited by Dr Patterson and by Dr Robinson, an Oldham practitioner. Although the doctors gave Edith morphia and bismuth, they soon concluded that she was a hopeless case. During the night, the vomiting continued.

At 7.00 a.m. on the Monday morning, Mrs Berry gave Edith a whitish substance which the girl was unable to swallow. Mrs Berry said: 'She cannot take it; her throat is made up.' Edith was continuously unwell throughout Monday and at around 5.00 a.m. on Tuesday January 4th, she died.

Because of the grave suspicion surrounding the death of the child, her stomach contents were examined. A inquest was held. During the examination and analysis, no direct poison was found. However, the doctors believed that death was due to the effect of a corrosive acidic substance. If it had been administered in diluted form during the Saturday and Sunday, no trace of it would be found by the Tuesday. The doctors thought that by the time of the post mortem, the acid would either have been absorbed by the body or ejected by the child's constant vomiting.

When exploring a possible motive for Mrs Berry's disposal of her child, her personal financial situation was considered. Mrs Berry had said that her daughter's life was not insured. However, on January 6th, only two days after Edith's death, she went to an insurance company and received ten pounds, a considerable sum in those days.

Mrs Berry's salary at the workhouse was £25 a year. This corresponded to a weekly income of less than ten shillings. Mrs Berry paid three shillings a week to Mrs Saunderson for Edith's maintenance, together with sixpence for her schooling, and a penny a week insurance. When the price of clothing was included, Edith was costing Mrs Berry about half of her salary. Moreover, in April 1886, Mrs Berry wanted to insure herself and her daughter for £100, but the proposal was unaccepted. She was not aware of the refusal when Edith died.

Elizabeth Berry was tried for murder over a period of five days in February 1887. Crown counsel McConnell told the jury that doctors believed that Edith Berry died from the effect of a corrosive irritant poison like sulphuric acid. There was a photograph taken of the child's face and body which was passed around the jury for their inspection. Mr McConnell drew the jury's attention to the extraordinary black marks on the dead girl's lips.

On the penultimate day of the trial, Mr Cottingham addressed the jury for the defence. He pointed out that up to the last moment of the girl's life, the doctors attending her treated the case as bleeding caused by inflammation of the stomach and bowels. (In reality, this was what had been happening, although there had been no mention of poisoning, at least not in official quarters.)

Mr McConnell told the jury that 'not one single vomit or towel was concealed by Mrs Berry.' He said: 'it was not until after the post mortem, which was made to clear up a difficult, doubtful, and obscure case, that they came to the conclusion that poison had been administered.' Ignoring the fact that acid in diluted form could have been employed, Mr McConnell claimed that 'if a corrosive acid had been used, the marks on the lips would have been seen at once, and not by only the Sunday night.'

Defence witness Thompson, an analytical chemist, said that acid, if used, would have been found in traces in the gullet and in the stomach. He also pointed out that Edith had tuberculosis and, being delicate, could easily have died from a stomach and bowel disorder.

In conclusion, Mr McConnell asked the jury: 'Why did the child not scream when the acid was poured into her mouth?' He also said: 'The accused's conduct was perfectly open.' She never, he claimed, refused access to the child. 'What motive was there which could transform this mother into a hideous and detestable monster?' The case for the prosecution had, he claimed, not been made out.

The jury did not accept Mr McConnell's defence arguments. They took only ten minutes to decide that Mrs Berry was guilty of murdering her child. Before being sentenced, Mrs Berry said: 'I may be charged, but the whole world cannot make me guilty.' Unfortunately for her, her guilt had already been proved.

In her petition to the Home Secretary, Mrs Berry said: 'If I did kill the child I am insane.' At first, she had blamed the medicine prescribed by Dr Patterson. It was believed in many quarters that a reprieve might be possible, as an act of royal clemency in the Queen's Golden Jubilee year. However, the execution went ahead on March 14th 1887.

Mrs Berry was the first person to be hanged at Walton Prison. Several changes had been made to the usual arrangements employed at Kirkdale. The gallows was built in a coach house which normally was used to protect the prison van from the weather. The drop was at floor level, thereby avoiding a climb to the scaffold, and beneath the trap door was a well over ten feet deep.

Mrs Berry wore the same black dress she wore at her trial. Snow lay an inch deep on the ground. When she saw the rope hanging down, she fainted. Two male prison officers placed her on the trap door. 'May the Lord have mercy upon me', she prayed. As the rope was adjusted around her neck, she said: 'May God forgive Dr Patterson.'

Hangman Berry carried out the execution without a hitch. Mrs Berry, who was only 4ft 9½in tall, was given a drop of 6ft 6in with a rope of diameter ¾inch. It was said that Mrs Berry knew her namesake the hangman, but it does seem very unlikely that they had ever met each other.

Stolen Goods

At the Liverpool Spring Assizes of 1890, William Chadwick, a 28-year-old labourer, was charged with the murder of Walter Davies, a pawnbroker's assistant, at Atherton on July 22nd 1889. Mr Watson led for the prosecution, Mr Sparrow for the defence. The judge was Mr Justice Mathew. Chadwick, who had in December 1889 been sentenced at Salford Sessions to five years penal servitude for a series of railway robberies, pleaded not guilty.

Walter Davies worked for a pawnbroker called John Lowe at a shop at 29 Market Street, Atherton. Every Saturday night when the shop closed for the weekend, Mr Lowe removed any valuable items and took them to his own house at 4 Market Street. Mr Davies would then take them back to the shop on Monday mornings.

On the Monday morning of July 22nd 1889, Walter Davies reached the shop, as usual, at 7 am. He had been told by Mr Lowe to clean and swill out the cellar. During the morning, Davies was seen stocking and cleaning the front shop window. Not long after, a neighbour, William Walker, saw Davies showing a man some silk handkerchiefs. However, Walker could not see who the man was because he had his back to the shop window.

At about 8.40 am, Mrs Jane Clews entered the shop and Davies was nowhere to be seen. She returned a few minutes later but Davies was still missing. She repeatedly called out, 'Walter!' but when she had no reply, Mrs Clews decided to look in the kitchen. It was here that she heard a choking noise coming from the cellar. Terrified, Mrs Clews ran to tell her husband and son. When they all returned, they found Mr Davies lying on the cellar floor. Large pools of blood stretched from the body to the cellar steps. Watches, jewellery and clothing had been stolen from the shop. Davies, battered and stabbed, had died from loss of blood, caused by the severing of the main vein in his neck.

A man called John Edward Lorn was charged with Davies' murder. However, after being put before the magistrates, he was discharged owing to a lack of evidence.

Suspicion then fell upon William Chadwick, a thief well known to the Lancashire police. Having a photograph of Chadwick on their files, they used it to track down his whereabouts. At about 7 am on the day of the murder, a knocker-up called Martha Gregory saw Chadwick walking along Kirkhall Lane. This lane ran between Leigh and Atherton. At about 8 am, a man resembling Chadwick approached a man called Stirrup in Atherton and asked him for a match. Stirrup noticed that the finger of the man's right hand was mutilated.

At the trial, other witnesses swore to having seen Chadwick that day in Atherton. Some of these witnesses were taken to Strangeways Prison to identify him.

When arrested, Chadwick was found to still be in possession of various items from the shop. Other valuables, including a watch and chain that Davies had been wearing when he was attacked, had been pawned by Chadwick at various shops in Liverpool and Manchester. He had used the names Fred Smith and Hampson amongst others. He was seen pawning Davies' watch in Manchester; another watch was pledged at Mrs Perry's shop on Brownlow Hill, Liverpool.

There was so much prosecution evidence against Chadwick that it took Crown counsel Watson two days to present it. There was little doubt that Chadwick would have had ample opportunity to commit the Atherton crime, and then spend most of the day in various local public houses where he was seen and recognised by numerous witnesses.

Summing up the prosecution evidence, Mr Watson told the jury that one of the watches, with its chain, was pledged by Chadwick. It belonged to the dead man and was worn by him on the morning of the murder. Chadwick was found with a large quantity of stolen goods from Lowe's shop. Mr Watson asked the jury: 'What could he be but the murderer?'

Mr Sparrow, for the defence, put forward a scenario that someone else had robbed the shop after Davies had been killed by an unknown enemy. He pointed out to the jury that the case depended very much on the identification of Chadwick as the killer. He said: 'The whole question is the most difficult one of identity.' Sparrow pointed out that Superintendent Weir had used a photograph for witnesses to identify, rather than giving them sight of Chadwick himself. 'This evidence,' said Sparrow, 'is tainted as a standpoint of conviction.' He asked, 'was it likely, that if the prisoner had committed the murder and pawned the goods, that he would have taken the police to the pawnshops and told them where the goods were pledged?' No blood was found on Chadwick. 'Why was not a scrap of bloodstained clothing produced?', he asked. Finally, he said, 'the whole of the circumstances are suspicious, but they are not, I contend, of the coherency which should lead you to say that the prisoner is beyond all doubt guilty.'

Mr Justice Mathew, in his summing up, dismissed the idea that someone else – during the excitement after the murder – came in and plundered the stock. Not only was the murdered man's watch taken, but Chadwick had admitted that he had previously pledged other articles as 'Smith' and 'Hampson' – the same names used when pawning the stolen property.

The jury retired at 2.15 pm on the third day. At 2.45 pm it returned with a guilty verdict. When the judge was about to pass sentence, Chadwick said he wished to make a statement which could be published in the newspapers. He had a speech defect, which had helped to identify him. He said: 'How a man like Millington (a prosecution witness) could swear I can speak for an hour without stammering, I do not know.' Continuing, Chadwick said:

> It is all spite. Superintendent Weir Sergeant Cragg pointed me out to witnesses in Strangeways. The whole of the evidence is a conspiracy against me. I am not afraid to die, but I want justice, and I have not had it. I have been a bad character. I have stolen hundreds of pounds worth, but I have done nothing further, and no-one can say he has ever seen me in bad company ... '

Here, his lordship interrupted Chadwick and said:

> I cannot grant you further indulgence. You cannot quarrel with the verdict of the jury nor can any reasonable man who has heard the evidence today ... Your learned counsel made every effort to relieve you of the load that hangs upon you pointing to that conclusion ... You were found in possession of the watch of the murdered man, and no-one can doubt that that watch was taken by your hand from his body.

'I am prepared at any time to die,' said Chadwick.

'Make use of the time that is left to you to sue God for mercy', replied the judge.

'I don't want Him, I want justice,' said Chadwick.

After sentence, he had to be dragged forcibly from the dock. He called out to his wife: 'Goodbye, Polly!'

Chadwick, on 14th April, had written a letter to his brother who lived at 54 John Street in Pendleton. The letter included the words: 'Dear brother, I have a lot to confess, but of the murder I am innocent'.

William Chadwick was hanged at Kirkdale Prison on 15th April 1890. The large open space that at one time was devoted to public executions was now almost covered with houses. Chadwick's place of execution was a small building inside the high prison wall. A door opened into the building from the prison corridor and a deep hole was bricked in the floor, some twelve feet deep and five feet wide. The hole was covered by the trap – a large folding shutter painted black. On the spot beneath the noose were two chalk marks to show where the criminal had to stand.

Just before the white hood was put over his head, Chadwick said to the chaplain: 'Give my love to my dear wife.' After the hood was placed over his head, Chadwick said: 'Goodbye, God bless you.' As the chaplain replied with 'God bless you', Berry withdrew the bolt, using a long-handled lever to release the trapdoor. The execution was carried out to perfection. Not a quiver shook the rope. A reporter said that the execution was 'short, sharp and merciful'.

Body Bag

On Tuesday 19th May 1891, at around 1 am, a dockgate man called Hugh Macdonald heard a splash in the Sandon Basin on the Liverpool waterfront. The tide had been ebbing since Monday evening and low water was expected that morning at about 2 am.

At this time, Macdonald saw a bundle floating in the water. An hour or so later, he realised in the half-light of dawn that the object was a sailor's kitbag that had two ensigns painted on it. With help from another dockgate man, John Irving and policeman Daniel Ellis, the bag was removed from the water.

Inside the bag they found two grey blankets, a large sharp knife, and a saw which appeared to have pieces of fat and bone marrow on its bloodstained teeth. At the bottom of the bag was the body of a boy. The throat had been cut from ear to ear and the legs cut off at the knees. The hands were in the small of the back as if they had been tied there. Constable Daniel Ellis searched the pockets and found a sixpence and a penny in the boy's trousers. Ellis took the body and the contents of the bag to the deadhouse on Prince's Dock.

The body was that of 10-year-old Nicholas Martin. He lived in Bridgewater Street with his mother, Ann Martin, who had last seen her son on 16th May, playing football near their house. Nicholas had his supper at about 6.30 pm – some egg, bread and tea. Mrs Martin first noticed him missing at about 10.30 pm on that Saturday night. She made inquiries in the neighbourhood, without success. She thought he may have gone to see an uncle in Great Howard Street, although when she went there on the Sunday, Nicholas was not there. After informing the police on Monday 18th, she was heartbroken to identify his dead body on the following day.

Police inquiries soon turned up a lead to the killer. On the night Nicholas was last seen by his mother, a man named Thomas Hankey had seen the boy in Bridgewater Street in the company of a man whom he recognised as John Conway, a 60-year-old marine fireman.

Hankey had seen Conway come out of a public house and speak to the boy.

'Come on if you are coming,' he shouted.

The boy replied: 'Wait while I get my ball.'

'Come on, never mind your ball, you will not want that any more.' Conway then gave the boy a sixpence and they both walked together up James Street, towards Stanhope Street. Conway was elderly and Hankey noticed that he wore a black jacket and trousers and had a white beard.

Curiously, about fourteen years previously, Conway had lodged in Mrs Martin's house, about four years before Nicholas was born. At the time of the boy's disappearance, Conway was lodging with Mrs Rose Ann Brown in Bridgewater Street.

John Conway was a delegate and secretary of the Sailors' and Firemen's Union. Although he usually resided with Mrs Brown, he also had the sole use of another house, at 19 Stanhope Street, which had three floors and an outside cellar. On the ground floor was an office where union business was transacted. The two upper rooms were unoccupied and unfurnished. The distance from Conway's lodgings to the house in Stanhope Street was only a few hundred yards.

On the night of Nicholas' disappearance, a man saw Conway carrying a pair of child's boots. When he asked Conway if he needed a cobbler, he told him he did not and passed by. Police searches later found some boots thrown over garden walls – one in Parliament Street and its pair in New Bird Street. Another pair of boots was found alongside a razor that Conway had taken from his lodgings.

Conway's landlady Mrs Brown often took charge of money for him. Monday 18th May was Whitsuntide Bank holiday and on the previous night, Conway had been to Mrs Brown to ask her for some money so that he could go on an excursion. She lent him a half sovereign, but he did not go away anywhere. Instead, he bought several items including a seaman's bag, two blankets, a knife, and a bucket, later found at the scene of the crime. He also bought a pennyworth of washing soda, which he used to clean a floor at his residence.

Conway was spotted transporting the boy's body from Stanhope Street to the Mersey waterfront. At the trial, evidence was given by Thomas Treanor, aged 16, who said that on the evening of Monday 18th May, he saw Conway coming out of Number 19 carrying a very large black bag. The bag seemed heavy and bumped awkwardly as Conway dragged it down the front steps of the building. Treanor asked Conway if he wanted help carrying the bag. He said he did not before putting it into a hansom cab. John Campbell, the cab driver, asked Conway if he would have the bag up on top of the cab. Conway replied: 'No, never mind, I will take it inside.' The driver then took him to the pier head near St George's baths, a relatively easy position for the easy disposal of the bag and its contents into the river.

In the period between the Whit Monday and his subsequent arrest, Conway complained to Mrs Brown that he felt unwell. On the Tuesday morning he had gone out early but soon returned, saying that he was ill. On the Wednesday he seemed very poorly; Mrs Brown noticed that he was shaking uncontrollably and sweating profusely.

In Stanhope Street, police searched the house and found in an oven, two labels which had been ripped from brown paper and used to wrap the body. Upstairs they found blood on two floorboards and dirt beneath the boards was soaked with blood.

Conway's two-day trial opened at St George's Hall on 31st July 1891. Crown counsel Mr Hopwood Q.C. and his junior Mr McConnell called some forty witnesses for the prosecution. At the close of the first day, the prosecution rested its case. The judge, Mr Justice Smith, said to the jury: 'I suggest that before being locked up for the night you should take a drive.'

On the second day of the trial, Saturday 1st August, defence counsel Segar addressed the jury on behalf of Conway. He said that someone else could have committed the murder, perhaps a foreign seaman. At the end of his speech to the jury, Mr Segar said:

> Is it credible that a man like the prisoner, who has retired from her Majesty's service with honour, a man always steady and of high repute, should have gone suddenly mad, should have committed a terrible murder, and should go about as if nothing bad happened? That a man could be for 61 years respectable, and then suddenly turn out a monster and not turn a hair afterwards – is that credible?

In his summing up, Mr Justice Smith said: 'Circumstantial evidence consists of a number of independent facts which tend to one point. If a fact be wanting, however, the prisoner is entitled to it, and to an acquittal by the law of England.'

The judge also said that the jury 'will have to decide whether the aggregation of testimony ... leads you to the irresistible conclusion that the man in the dock is guilty of the murder of the boy'. He pointed out that 'there has been no malpractice to the boy'. Conway was a well respected man who had served his country. 'If someone else had murdered the boy in Stanhope Street, why did Conway not go to the police and tell them?'

A long denial of the crime by Conway was read out by Herbert Stephen, Clerk of Assize. Conway blamed a foreign sailor. He pointed out that at 1 am when the splash was heard, Mrs Brown had confirmed that he was at home in bed.

The jury took half an hour to find Conway guilty as charged. A large crowd surrounded the north exit of St George's Hall when he was taken by two warders in a cab to Kirkdale.

The execution of John Conway on Thursday 20th August 1891 was the last to be carried out at Kirkdale. Thereafter, all Liverpool hangings were held, until the very last one in 1964, at Walton Prison.

As hangman Berry was drawing the white cap over Conway's face, he called out: 'Hold on, man, hold on! I want to say something.'

'There is no time now.' Berry replied. Father Bonte intervened so Conway continued: 'Beware of drink,' He hesitated, and then declared: 'I want to speak to the officials of the prison, that they were kind to me and by God'. As if trying to postpone the inevitable, he cried out: 'Oh Lord! Lord! Lord! May God have mercy on my soul! Oh my God, my God!'

While Conway was still speaking, Berry drew back the lever. Conway's head was almost ripped from his body. Only his neck muscles prevented decapitation and blood started to drip to the floor. A drop of six feet had proved to have been too great. Immediately after Conway had been despatched, a letter of confession, signed by Conway on the morning ofhis death, was read out by Father Bonte:

> I accept the sentence that has been pronounced against me as just, and I now offer my life in satisfaction to all whom I have offended, to God, to my religion, to my country, to the parents of the victim, to the victim himself, and to society. In confessing my guilt, I protest that my motive was not outrage. Such a thought I never in all my life entertained. Drink has been my ruin, not lust. I was impelled to the crime while under the influence of drink by a fit of murderous mania, and a morbid curiosity to observe the process of dying. A moment after the commission of the crime I experienced the deepest horror of it, and would have done anything in the world to undo it. May God in his mercy forgive me.

Child Killer

At about 1.20 pm in the afternoon of Tuesday 8th November 1892, a woman called Martha Hindle was on her way to a funeral. She was passing a gate leading into Witton Park, Blackburn, when she found the body of a 9-year-old girl called Alice Barnes. Alice was the daughter of a farmer at Redlam, near Blackburn. She was tall for her age and very intelligent. On weekday mornings she attended school, returning home at about 12.30 pm, when she would help her parents on the farm.

One of Alice's duties was to collect their nine cows and lead them over a footbridge and through a wicket gate onto the grass of Witton Park.

Eye-witnesses helped to trace Alice's movements that Tuesday afternoon. She had left the farmhouse just before 1 pm to tend to the cows, accompanied by her younger sister Mary as far as the bridge which crossed over a stream. Several children saw a man standing on the footbridge, who was later believed to have been Alice's killer. One of them was 12-year-old Elizabeth Riding, the daughter of the head gamekeeper of Witton Park; the other was 12-year-old Edith Duxbury. Both of the girls had said the man just stood there staring at them.

Just as the one o'clock gun was fired, the cattle were being driven by Alice through the open gate. Elizabeth noticed that the man had now left the bridge, and Alice, having guided the cattle into the pasture, was returning towards the gate. Elizabeth's younger brother Harry, aged 10, had seen the man pass through the gate carrying a child in his arms. The man then dropped the child on to the floor in the same spot where Alice's body was later found. Harry saw the man run across the bridge and up Spring Lane, as far as Grimshaw's corner, where he was spotted at 1.10 pm. He then went down the Blackburn Road, turned into a passage and entered a cul-de-sac. When he was forced to turn back, he was seen by several more people, before he disappeared completely.

The Blackburn Police carefully examined the body and the crime scene. They noticed signs of a struggle on the ground near the wicket gate, and in the soft mud there was a boot print of which a plaster cast was taken.

Alice Barnes had been suffocated by a handkerchief that had been pushed down her throat. Lying on the floor next to the wicket, her body was covered in mud and her clothes had been disarranged. Blood had issued from her mouth and there was more blood on the girl's legs.

Several local men were arrested on suspicion of her murder and were interviewed by the police. On Sunday 13th November, five days after the murder, Superintendent Myers and two constables went to the house of Cross Duckworth, a brass finisher and native of Blackburn, who had also served in the army in India. He lived at a house in Primrose Terrace in Blackburn with his wife and two children.

When Duckworth opened the door to the police officers he immediately said: 'You haven't come about the murder, have you?', even though they had said a word about it. He was taken to the police station where he made a signed statement. He said he had left home on Tuesday 8th November at 7 am and had visited several public houses. A little before 9.30 am he went to a coal siding and met his brother before going with him to deliver a load of coal. He said they left the Dun Horse at 12.20 pm and went straight home along Griffin Street. He alleged that his children were at home when he arrived back, but they told the police that they had not seen their father at all. Furthermore, according to Duckworth's brother, the coal delivery had taken place on a different day.

Duckworth's alibi was soon discredited. He had been recognised at various places in Blackburn as well as at the crime scene. At about 11 am that morning, he was seen in the Unicorn in Throstle Street, where he drank several glasses of porter. He stayed there until about 12.40 pm and then called at the Turner's Arms for a small bottle of soda water. He was then seen at the Griffin, before walking up Redlam Brow. When the murder was committed, he was a few minutes' walk from the crime scene. He was also identified as being the man seen at the Witton Park wicket gate and footbridge. In addition, the boot print matched one of Duckworth's boots and the fatal handkerchief was similar to two found in his house.

Cross Duckworth's murder trial opened at Liverpool on 12th December 1892. Duckworth pleaded not guilty. The judge was Mr Justice Grantham.

At the end of the first day of the trial, Dr O'Feeley completed the case for the prosecution. The next morning defender Mr McKeand announced that he would be calling witnesses on behalf of Duckworth. He presented an alibi defence and sought to establish that near the time of the murder, five men were talking to Duckworth on the corner of a street about three quarters of a mile from the scene of the crime. McKeand also called witnesses to oppose the prosecution evidence about the boots Duckworth was wearing, and the evidence of the plaster cast made by the police. As a result, the judge instructed the jury to disregard any evidence about the boots and the cast of the muddy boot-print.

Addressing the jury, Mr McKeand asked if it could really rely on the evidence of young children that had been presented by the prosecution. He claimed that when the one o'clock gun was fired, Duckworth was talking to friends some distance from the crime scene. The prisoner, claimed McKeand, 'looked like the man on the footbridge, but that was all.'

In his peroration, Mr McKeand said to the jury: 'The spirit of that little child is crying aloud for vengeance. The hands of all men are raised against the miscreant who has done the deed, and throughout the length and breadth of this country there is a merciless cry for the blood of that man.'

Finally, Mr McKeand said: 'It would be better that this crime, detestable and cruel as it is, should go unpunished, that the bright and shining altars of justice should be stained and saturated with innocent blood.'

When Dr O'Feeley had reviewed the prosecution evidence, Mr Justice Grantham summed up. The judge said that he believed the motive was violation of the girl, but this had been prevented by the appearance of the lad who gave evidence. 'The great difficulty the jury has to face is the fact that proof of the prisoner being the man on the bridge, rests almost exclusively upon the testimony of children.'

The jury retired at 5.30 pm and returned after an hour with a guilty verdict, accompanied by a recommendation to mercy on the grounds that Duckworth's primary objective was not murder.

The morning of the execution on 3rd January was dark and cold and there was a sprinkling of snow on the ground from the previous night. The executioner was James Billington and as usual, the reporters were not allowed to witness the hanging. The prison governor at Walton announced that the sentence had been carried out 'promptly and skilfully without the slightest hitch'.

Deadly Affair

In 1894, John Walber, aged 55, had been married to his wife, Margaret, for five years. They lived at 4 Gildart Street in Liverpool, where Margaret ran a grocery shop. John was a French polisher. At five feet two inches in height, Walber was several inches shorter than his wife. They had an unhappy marriage and were both addicted to alcohol.

In 1877, twelve years before they got married, John Walber had lived for about three weeks with a woman called Ann Connolly. In 1894 when Connolly was living in Oakes Street, Walber returned to live with her, but when Ann discovered that he was now a married man, she turned him out of the house.

Seventeen years had elapsed since John Walber's brief indiscretion. Nevertheless, when Margaret discovered that John had visited Ann again she was so furious that she subjected him to a series of dreadful punishments which culminated in his eventual death.

On May 2nd, 1894, when John was walking to Ann's house, his wife followed and attacked him. Ann told John to leave and Margaret began punching her husband, shouting: 'You can keep him!'

However, from that day until his death six months later, John Walber was imprisoned by his wife in an upper room at 4 Gildart Street. The others lodgers in the house said that over the six month period they had only seen Walber twice. Margaret told lodger Nancy Hannan that she kept John upstairs in case he went to 'a bad house in Oakes Street'. Margaret said: 'I will have to give the old bugger a flypaper'. Walber's clothes were taken away and put into the cellar and the door of his bedroom was kept fastened with a lock and chain. Lodgers and neighbours frequently heard the sounds of scuffling and Walber calling out: 'Murder!'

On Sunday 12th November, lodger Mary Vauze heard Walber say: 'Oh, Maggie, I will not go there any more'. Margaret told her that John was blind and paralysed and 'would not leave the house until he was carried out in a coffin'.

On Monday 13th November, Walber was visited by his sister Elizabeth. She said that he was naked except for a dark-coloured shirt and he seemed dazed and incoherent. Elizabeth suggested bringing in a doctor or a clergyman to attend to John, but Margaret would not allow it. 'You will fetch no-one here', she said. Margaret also claimed that Walber's illness was 'all mockery'. She told Elizabeth: 'One week he pretends to be paralysed. Another week he pretends to be blind'. Although Walber heard these comments, he remained silent.

On the morning of the 15th November, Margaret said once again, 'I have good mind to give him a flypaper'. Her son John Murray, who also lived at Gildart Street, replied: 'Don't do that to the poor old man'. The same day, in a public house, Margaret told a friend, Ellen Mottram: 'I would give a sovereign if the windows of Annie Connolly were smashed. I have already served five years and can do another ten.'

The next morning, matters came to a head. Margaret was drunk and she went into Mary Vauze's room and said to her: 'My son has killed John. John is dead.' Holding a cloth in her hand, she then continued: 'I don't think he is dead. I will go and wipe the blood off his face'. When Vauze realised that Walber really was dead, she went with Margaret and another lodger, James Pearson, to the detective office.

Margaret's son John Murray had found Walber's body lying on the floor of the top room, in a dreadful condition. Pieces of the jug and basin chamberware lay around the room. The bedclothes were scattered. Blood covered the sheets, pillow, floor and walls. He had not killed his stepfather, although to everyone else, it seemed as if he had, because shortly afterwards he had fled to Dublin. Margaret had drawn four pounds from a savings bank, given it to her son and advised him to make himself scarce. Panicking, Murray made off to Garston, and then ultimately found his way to Dublin, where he was later arrested. He became a prosecution witness against his mother.

At the detective office Margaret admitted the crime. She said: 'I hit him on the head with a chair. John had nothing to do with it.' In a statement to Detective Inspector Bryson, Margaret said she had gone to her husband's room, after she realised that Walber had her son's trousers on. She took the chain off the door and hit her husband on the head with it. She finished by saying: 'I do not remember what else I did because I was drunk at the time.'

A post mortem examination was performed by Dr Kellett Smith. He reported that Walber was well nourished but there were wounds and bruises on the face, head, arms and body. Some had been caused by kicks, others by a sharp instrument. Part of the man's beard had been cut off and the missing portion was found in the room. The doctor also noticed some glass in one or two of the wounds, which he though had been caused by a blow inflicted with a lamp-glass. He concluded that death was due to shock and blood loss.

Mrs Walber was tried for murder at the Spring Assizes. The judge was Mr Justice Day and for the Crown was Mr McConnell. The defence was handled by Dr Commins M.P. In his address to the jury, Dr Commins said that there was 'no direct evidence that the prisoner took the life of her husband.' This statement implied that the murderer was John Murray. Commins also submitted that the blood on Mrs Walber's clothes proved nothing, because the pools of blood covering the floor could have easily soaked into her dress whilst she was in the room.

Mr Justice Day ruled out manslaughter. He said: 'It is murder or nothing.' The jury took fifteen minutes to return the guilty verdict.

When asked if she had anything to say to why sentence of death should not be passed, Mrs Walber replied: 'I am not guilty, my Lord'. While the judge was pronouncing the sentence, she cried out: 'Oh, my Lord, I am innocent of killing my husband!' She was removed to the cells in the care of a female warder.

On a foggy Monday morning, in April 1894, Margaret Walber was executed on the gallows at Walton Prison. The black flag was raised at 8.03 am and, as usual, the press was kept away from the actual hanging. On the prison gate there was a certificate, signed by the medical officer, by Governor Walker, and by Chaplain Father Wade, confirming that Margaret Walber had been duly executed in their presence.

Attended by Matron Miss Gee and several female officers, Mrs Walber walked with a steady step. On her way to the gallows, she neither confessed nor denied the crime.

The hangman was James Billington. According to custom, the body was allowed to hang for an hour, after which it was cut down and removed to the prison mortuary to await the official inquest, which traditionally opened at 10 am.

A Hot Temper

In the spring of 1894, John Langford, a baker aged 41, was living with 21-year-old Elizabeth Stephen at 110 Cockerell Street, off Liverpool's Walton Road. They had been living together for the past four years even though Langford was not divorced from his wife. It was not known where his wife was and whether or not she was still alive. The cohabiting couple lived with Langford's three children, aged 10, 13 and 15. The couple were both alcoholics and Langford was a hot-tempered man. When the couple had been drinking they often quarrelled. One of their drunken confrontations was to have very tragic consequences.

On the morning of Tuesday 3rd April 1894, Lizzie Stephen visited her neighbour, Jane Sharp, at 109 Barry Street. Lizzie and Jane went with a woman called Smith, for a drink at a pub on the corner of Fountains Road. Then they returned to 110 Cockerell Street and drank some more.

At about 12.40 pm, the three drinking companions went outside, hoping to see a funeral pass by, but unfortunately the cortege had already gone. They decided to go into Cain's public house at the corner of Florence Street and Walton Lane, where they arrived just before 1 pm.

The women had scarcely got inside the pub when Langford, on seeing Lizzie, struck her with his fist on the side of her face. Manager Frank Lennon jumped over the counter and ordered them out of the premises. Lizzie walked away, closely followed by Langford. In an entry behind Cockerell Street, he caught up with Lizzie and plunged a knife into her chest, before attempting to commit suicide by cutting his own throat. At Stanley Hospital, before she died, Lizzie Stephen said: 'I was drunk. I don't know if he was or not. The cause of it was my own fault'.

Just four weeks after the fatal stabbing, John Langford came up for trial before Mr Justice Day and a jury. As well as being accused of murder, Langford was charged with the crime of attempted suicide.

Background evidence was given by Langford's daughter Mary, aged 13. She said that Lizzie Stephen had been drinking from Easter Monday, 26th March, until the day of the stabbing on Tuesday 3rd April. Her father had been drinking too, and in reply to Mr McConnell, Crown prosecutor, Mary said she had heard her father say on three separate occasions that he would swing for Lizzie.

Mary said that on the night of April 2nd, Lizzie was drunk and slept all night on the hearthrug in the kitchen. When Mary got up next morning, Lizzie had gone out, so she went to school with the other two children, leaving the house key with a neighbour.

When Mary returned home at 12.30 pm Lizzie was still not home. At about 1.30 pm she heard a noise in the entry and when she went to investigate, Mary Langford found Lizzie and her father on the ground. They had by now both sustained stab wounds.

William Emery, aged 8, of Barry Street, was in the back entry at about 1.30 pm. He saw Langford chasing Lizzie down the entry, brandishing a knife. Langford caught hold of her by the back of her dress, turned her around, and stabbed her in the chest, striking downwards. He then walked up the entry and wiped the knife blade on a wall. After being stabbed, Lizzie ran a few yards and then fell to the ground. William said that Langford then shut the knife, put it into his trouser pocket and started walking towards him, so he fled for his life.

Another young lad who witnessed the stabbing was John Shaughnessy, who resided in Cockerell Street. He saw Langford strike Lizzie in the chest before she fell on to her back. Langford looked down at her, covered his eyes with his hands and then looked down at her again. He got hold of his whiskers with his left hand and drew a knife across his throat two or three times before falling down on to the woman.

A woman called Mary Kennedy asked Lizzie: 'What has he done to you?' She replied: 'The pig!' After cutting his throat, Langford was heard to say: 'We will die together'. Another witness heard him say: 'I said I would swing for you, and I will.'

Police Constable Evans gave first aid at the scene and then had the couple taken to the Stanley Hospital. Detective Constable Casey heard Langford say: 'Lizzie, are you not dead yet?' He also used a good deal of foul language. Casey asked him why he had stabbed the woman to which Langford replied: 'For her unfaithfulness to me'. At the hospital Langford also said: 'Put the ***** beside me and let us die together'.

Lizzie Stephen had received a wound to her lung that was one and a half inches long and two inches deep. After giving depositions to a magistrate's clerk from her sick bed, she died from shock and blood loss.

Langford was defended by Mr Collingwood Hope. In his final address he told the jury that Lizzie had said: 'The cause of the quarrel was pawning and also drinking'. Mr Hope pointed out that Langford had only stabbed her once before cutting his own throat. Hope said: 'Does this not appear to be the act of a repentant passionate man?' He asked the jury for verdict of manslaughter.

The judge, in his summing up, said: 'There is not a shadow of doubt that the woman died at the hands of the prisoner. She had lived with him under circumstances not recognised by the law and in respect of which the law gave him no rights. The jury was to disregard her unfaithfulness.' Finally, Mr Justice Day said: 'I cannot conceive that there is anything whatever to reduce the offence from wilful murder to manslaughter'.

The jury spent the time between 3 pm and 3.20 pm in consultation. Its guilty verdict was accompanied by a strong recommendation to mercy. Throughout the trial, Langford had been distraught had expressed deep regret for his crime. He was crying whilst his daughter Mary gave evidence, and he was removed from the desk ashen-faced, in an apparent state of shock.

After the regulatory three Sundays had elapsed following the death sentence, John Langford was brought to execution at Walton on Tuesday 22nd May 1894. It was carried out in a wooden shed in the prison yard. On the night before, Langford was said to have gone to bed early and slept well.

Just before he was hanged, Langford received Holy Communion in the prison chapel. Anglican Chaplain Reverend D. Morris officiated. As was usual, the victim approached the gallows and the chaplain recited the litany for the dying, which included the words: 'I am the resurrection and the Life'.

The sombre procession took only two minutes from the condemned cell to the gallows. Then there was only a minute's delay on the scaffold. James Billington was the hangman.

It was announced that Langford's three children had been admitted to the Dr Bernado's Homes. On the night before his execution they were sent to the London Homes, so that they were far away from the proximity of their father's crime.

The Trapdoor

William Miller was a Liverpudlian sailor who worked on the Woodside ferry boats. Although he was married with several children, on the 24th October 1894 he went to America with another woman. Shortly before Christmas of that year he returned to his father-in-law's house at 61 Edgeware Street, Edge Hill, where he and his wife lived. Unfortunately, his erstwhile lady friend turned up and caused trouble, forcing Miller to flee to Edinburgh.

On the 7th February 1895, Miller returned to Liverpool and went to live in the Great Charlotte Street cocoa rooms. He left there on the morning of Monday 18th February. The next day, Miller killed a man called Edward Moyse.

Moyse, a homosexual aged 52, kept a bookstall on Mann Island, near the Liverpool pierhead where he sold second-hand and antiquarian books. He lived in an apartment at 26 Redcross Street, above a barber's shop run by a man called Carter.

On the 2nd February, 15-year-old John Needham, spoke to Moyse about an advertisement he had seen for an assistant. The next day, Needham's father went to see Moyse at Redcross Street, and his visit resulted in the young lad being appointed on a month's trial, for two shillings a week. John Needham moved into Moyse's apartment on the 3rd February.

On Monday 18th February, Moyse closed up his bookstall at about 5.45 pm, and directed Needham to move a load of books to Redcross Street. He finished transporting them at about 6.30 pm whilst Moyse was out of the house, buying some more books.

At 6.45 pm, William Miller came to the house and asked to see Moyse. Needham told him that he would not return home until about 9 pm. Miller explained to Needham that he had come to buy some valuable books and would come back later. He returned early, at 8 pm.

According to Needham, Mr Miller entered the house and sat down opposite him by the fire.

'Moyse is queer, isn't he?' Miller asked. 'The way he walks and talks is awfully queer'.

'It is'. The boy replied.

Miller then asked the boy where Moyse kept his money, to which he said that he did not know.

'It is very queer he does not tell you where his money is, or where his relations are.'

Needham took out his watch. 'This is the watch my father gave me.'

'It is a nice little one'. Miller took the watch in his hand. He then asked Needham if he knew whether Moyse had a bank, adding: 'I will bring you a parrot the next time I come home from sea.'

Just then, Moyse entered the room. They shook hands and he said to Miller, 'I did not expect you here so soon.' Moyse explained to the young lad that Miller was a previous lodger of his.

'He will sleep on the sofa tonight.' Moyse said. 'Tomorrow you can make up the bed in the best room for him.'

After being told to go to bed, Needham left Moyse and Miller together in the kitchen.

The next morning, Needham rose at 5 am. He lit a candle and walked into the scullery. Miller was carrying a bucket and hatchet, and asked the boy where the coal was kept. He showed Miller where the coal was before returning to his bedroom. Miller went up to the boy's room and pointed out a trapdoor over the landing that led to the attic. The boy suggested it was a manhole. Miller used a chair to reach into the hole and rooted about in an apparent search for hidden cash. He then went back downstairs and Needham returned to his bedroom.

A few minutes later, Miller crept back upstairs, blew out the candle, and struck the boy on the head with a poker. Needham found himself at the bottom of the stairs and Miller struck him again. The boy seized Miller by the legs, but Miller pushed him away and began to strangle him. Miller warned, 'If you follow me, I will come back and kill you.'

After Miller had left the house, Needham went into Moyse's room, and found him beaten, his pillow and head covered in blood. The terrified boy fled into the street, bleeding from various head wounds.

A passing dockgate man called Corran found Needham and summoned the police. The boy was seriously injured and in shock and was taken to the Northern Hospital.

When the police arrived at 26 Redcross Street they found evidence of a violent struggle in Edward Moyse's bedroom. The man was deceased, lying on the bed, with horrendous wounds on his head and face. The pillow was soaked in blood and pools of it were on the floor and around the fireplace. The doctor who examined Moyse said that he had been dead for about an hour.

On the day of the murder, Miller was sighted in South Castle Street at around 9 am by Catherine Davies. Miller told her that the night before, at 10 pm, he had been in Redcross Street and had seen four men and four women at the door of Number 26. Catherine said to him, 'It was not done at ten last night. It was done between five and six in the morning.'

Later that day, Miller went back home to Edgeware Street and changed his underclothes. When his mother-in-law drew his attention to the blood on his waistcoat, he rubbed the stains with a damp cloth and said he had been working in an abattoir.

Miller remained with his wife until, on the morning of Friday 22nd February, he was arrested and charged with murder by Detective Inspector Fisher. Miller used the same excuse to explain his blood-stained clothing. He told Fisher that he had been 'cutting up livers in an abattoir'. From his sick-bed, Needham positively identified Miller as the man who had attacked him.

Miller, in a statement, declared that he didn't know Edward Moyse aside from having seen him at his bookstall. He said that on the night of the killing, he had been walking all night around Liverpool looking for work.

At the house in Redcross Street, the police found a bloodstained poker on the kitchen table and a hatchet, also bloodstained, was found in Needham's bed. Dr Paul, a professor at Liverpool Victoria University, carried out the autopsy, and attributed death to a fractured skull. Paul said that the fatal wounds were probably inflicted by 'a square-headed instrument like a hatchet'.

Miller's murder trial was held over a period of three days in May 1895. Mr Justice Hawkins presided. Miller's defence counsel, Mr Ross Brown, did not dispute any of the prosecution evidence. However, he claimed that it was a case of mistaken identity and that the police had got the wrong man.

Mr Justice Hawkins summed up the evidence for 2½ hours on the third day of the trial. He told the jury that it should 'consider the boy Needham to be an intelligent, honest and trustworthy witness'. The judge also told them that they might 'draw the inference that the man who was at Redcross Street the night before the crime was the man who committed the crime the following morning'. It took the jury twenty minutes to find Miller guilty. After being sentenced to death, he was removed in a van and horses at the back of St George's Hall, thereby preventing any public demonstration.

William Miller's solicitor, W.H. Quilliam, tried to obtain a reprieve, but without success. As a result, Miller's execution went ahead as scheduled on Tuesday 4th June 1895. On the previous afternoon, Miller had been visited by his wife and her new-born baby. A collection for Mrs Miller raised only £1 11s 8½d.

On the morning of his execution, there was a cloudless blue sky and bright sunshine at Walton Prison. A drop of seven feet five inches was provided by hangman James Billington, assisted by William Warbrick. Miller protested his innocence until his last breath.

The Last Hanging

The last person to be hanged at Liverpool in the 1800s was Thomas Lloyd, a 55-year-old boilermaker. On 19th June 1897, Lloyd murdered his wife in their apartment at 39 Tillard Street, Liverpool.

Thomas and Julia Ann Lloyd had a very unhappy life together. They occupied the first floor at number 39, and a couple called Mr and Mrs McDowell had rooms in the same building. On many occasions Mrs McDowell intervened and tried to make peace between the warring couple.

On Saturday 19th June, Lloyd had a disagreement with Julia and left the house. He returned shortly before 11 pm, and from her bed, Mrs McDowell heard the Lloyds quarrelling downstairs. Mrs Lloyd was using a lot of bad language. At last the dispute seemed to have ended, when Julia said: 'I will go to bed'.

Mrs McDowell heard Julia climb the staircase and go into a small bedroom. Later, Lloyd also came upstairs and shouted to his wife, 'I will kill you, and the other one too!'

Lloyd then went downstairs but returned soon afterwards and walked along the lobby towards Mrs McDowell's room. He opened the door and looked in, but did not enter. Mrs McDowell had noticed that he was carrying a hatchet. Thomas then went to the door of his wife's bedroom.

Mrs McDowell, in the light from an oil lamp in her room, got out of bed and could see Lloyd leaning into his wife's doorway. To Mrs McDowell's astonishment, he then proceeded to strike Julia's head four or five times with the hatchet. As the blows reigned down he shouted: 'I'll cut the head off you!'

The next morning, a frightened Mrs McDowell found Julia unconscious. On the advice of a doctor, Mrs Lloyd was taken to hospital. Not once coming out of her comatose condition, she eventually died in hospital on the 26th June.

When, on 24th June, Lloyd was arrested, he told Constable 258E: 'I did it. I have to be hung. I will swing like a man.' However, when he was charged with the attempted murder of his wife, Lloyd replied: 'No, never. I never struck her. No-one ever saw me strike her.'

Thomas Lloyd was tried before Mr Justice Bruce and a jury at the Summer Assizes. For the prosecution, evidence was heard from Mr and Mrs Gray of Chelmsford Street. Mrs Gray said that late on the Saturday night in question, Lloyd, who was drunk, told her that he was afraid to go home, in case his wife would not let him into the house. The Grays went with Lloyd to Tillard Street and there, the Lloyds started to shout at each other. The next day, Mrs Gray saw Julia, and in a period of brief consciousness, she told her that Thomas had inflicted her injuries 'with his hand'.

Mr Gray testified that after the tragedy, Lloyd had said to him: 'I have very nearly killed the old woman. I think I have struck the fatal blow this time.'

The condition of Mrs Lloyd's body was described in evidence. There were four separate wounds on the left side of the head. Two of the wounds, above the left ear, had each penetrated the bone and fractured the skull. Death was attributed to blood loss arising from a laceration of the brain.

Mr Dowdall, defending, said that death had resulted merely as a result of a drunken quarrel. He said: 'Subject to the direction of his lordship, you may infer that there was no deliberate attempt to murder her.'

After twenty minutes of consultation, the jury reached its guilty verdict. After being given the automatic death sentence, Lloyd walked calmly and quietly to the cells below.

Thomas Lloyd was hanged by James Billington at Walton on Wednesday 18th August 1897. This was the last Liverpool hanging of the century. By 8 am, around a hundred spectators were outside the prison, standing in the heavy rain. When the black flag was raised, a murmur rippled through the crowd. Many remarked: 'He has gone'. Later that morning, the following customary notice was affixed to the prison door:

We the undersigned hereby declare that the judgement of death was
this day executed on Thomas Lloyd in her Majesty's Prison of Liverpool,
in our presence:- Dated the 18th day of August 1897. Signed:-
Henry L. Wright, Under-Sheriff of Lancashire
Miles J. Walker, Governor of said prison
D. Morris, Chaplain of said prison